THE WOUNDED

WHO WOULD A TEACHER BE?

Other titles in the Wounded Pilgrim Series
edited by Brian Thorne

GRACE ABOUNDING
Dorin Barter

THE FULCRUM AND THE FIRE
Susan Walrond-Skinner

THE DARK UNCERTAINTY
Sarah and David Clark

TO TRAVEL HOPEFULLY
Anthony Faulkner

WHO WOULD A TEACHER BE?

WRESTLING WITH RELIGIOUS EDUCATION

Clare Richards

DARTON · LONGMAN + TODD

First published 1994 by
Darton, Longman and Todd Ltd
1 Spencer Court
140–142 Wandsworth High Street
London SW18 4JJ

ISBN 0–232–52052–6

A catalogue record for this book is available
from the British Library

Abbreviations used are as follows:
JB The Jerusalem Bible
RSV Revised Standard Version
GNB Good News Bible

Cover design by Sarah John

Phototypeset in $10\frac{1}{2}$/13pt Bembo by Intype, London
Printed and bound in Great Britain
at the University Press, Cambridge

This book is for
all pilgrims
but especially for Fr Bill
who inspired
the last chapter.

CONTENTS

Foreword by Brian Thorne vii

Preface ix

Introduction 1

1. Making a New Start 9
2. Feed the World 25
3. Trespassers Will Be Forgiven 48
4. Growing Up 71
5. By Whose Authority? 93
6. God is Love 116
7. You Did It Unto Me 137

Postscript: The Pilgrim's Way 157

Notes 163

FOREWORD

The 'Wounded Pilgrim' series is inspired by the belief that spiritual growth demands an openness to experience and a willingness to accept the challenge of self-knowledge despite the suffering, confusion and agony of spirit which this can involve.

Each author in the series has agreed to take the risk of exposing his or her vulnerability and inner struggle so that others may find comfort and support as they, too, seek the courage to continue on their own spiritual pilgrimage. The books are offered as nourishment for the many seekers in our society who yearn for understanding and encouragement but have all too often experienced the bewilderment or even the hostility of their co-religionists in the institutional Churches. Each writer in his or her own way attempts to respond to the call for a decade of evangelism or evangelization but does so out of the pain and woundedness which almost invariably accompany the determination to be true to experience. There is no spirit of crusading or triumphalism to be found in these pages but rather the paradoxically fragile resilience of those who have not allowed their fear to prevent them entering the eye of the storm.

Clare Richards writes as one who daily puts herself on the line and dares to confront the unpredictable challenges and questions of adolescents in the classroom. She does so as a teacher who tries to remain faithful to the Roman Catholic Church, despite the inner turbulence and even anguish which such fidelity often causes her. That is not to say that her attitude towards the Church is one of truculent rebellion or reluctant submission.

Continually she seeks to hold the tension between what experience tells her and what the Church appears to require of a teacher of religious education in a Catholic comprehensive school.

The account of her struggle and her unwavering search for truth throws into relief the almost intolerable responsibility which is borne by teachers who care deeply not only about the minds of their students but also about their hearts and souls. What is more, the responsibility can be a lonely one. Academic colleagues often do not understand the level of personal risk which is involved for the religious education teacher while church friends or pastors may regard him or her as in some way 'unsound' or 'heretical' or, at best, 'misguided'. It is my hope that Clare Richards by her courage in writing about her own struggles and conflicts will offer companionship to many others for whom the task of introducing young people to religious knowledge and experience means a daily questioning of their own beliefs and a preparedness to be changed by their encounter with those who are quick to spot the merest hint in inauthenticity. For teachers in the post-*Veritatis Splendor* period and in the face of the surging tide of fundamentalism in many parts of the world, the task is unlikely to become less demanding in the times ahead.

BRIAN THORNE

PREFACE

Last week one of my students asked me why I taught RE rather than another subject. Good question! I began my teaching career as a PE teacher. I changed to RE because my own faith journey took on more importance than anything else. My spiritual pilgrimage is bound up in my teaching experience. The one has always fed the other.

When Brian Thorne invited me to contribute to the 'Wounded Pilgrim' series I hesitated at first, wondering if my life pilgrimage had anything to offer to fellow travellers. It only took a cup of coffee and an hour's reflection to realize that he was offering me a wonderful chance to open up for others the tensions that exist for Christians who feel called to share their belief with others. In this decade of evangelism, it is perhaps a good time to take a look at the role of teacher/pilgrim. Over recent years this role has undergone some pretty deep changes, and for many of us this has been a bruising and a battering experience. I welcome this opportunity to sort out for myself, and to share with you, why and how my understanding of theology, that is, of my relationship with God, has developed.

A Christian pilgrim is on a journey which is signposted 'to God'. But as God is the mystery that can never be fully grasped, Christians have always sought for reminders of God to take them along the right road. Some Christians call these reminders sacraments. The first of these is, of course, Jesus himself. In my Roman Catholic tradition we celebrate a further seven sacraments

– or signposts pointing through Christ to God. I have taken these signs as the groundplan for my writing. Signposts are rather important for pilgrims and travellers.

INTRODUCTION

It is eight o'clock on a Monday morning in December. I am shouting to my daughter to hurry up and come out of the bathroom. Why does it take her twenty minutes when the rest of us manage in five? My son suddenly remembers he didn't collect the last of his sponsor money and it is due in this morning. I agree to lend him the outstanding two pounds – only to find I haven't any change. Why is there always a pre-school breakfast-time chaos? My husband Bert says we don't get up early enough. I suspect he is right but I really couldn't manage on less sleep.

We grab school bags, handbag, PE kit and saxophone and go out to the car. It's frosty. I groan with agitation: another delay and I must be in school within fifteen minutes for staff briefing. If we don't leave now we catch the heavy queues. Bert eventually drops us at the school gate and I rush in reaching the staff-room just as Sr Mary has greeted my companions. They are all laughing. I have missed the joke, but at least I am in time for the messages which keep a large comprehensive school running more or less smoothly.

Today's contributions are typical. There is a new school governor on site all day. Year-9 reports are due in this week; Year-11 anticipated exam grades should have been completed last week. A practice will take place for Senior Orchestra and Wind Band after lunch to extend into periods 5 and 6. Pupils who missed language mock orals will be interviewed this afternoon in Room 53 (sixth-form RE room). The small hall is not in use all week because of the sixth-form pantomime. Congratulations are due to the Under-14 Netball Team who won the County Cup beating old rivals, City High. We end our briefing with a prayer. Today one of the English department reads a poem about stillness and reflection.

Fifteen minutes until my first class. I'm not a form tutor as I am a part-timer (just). This gives me time to clear the main corridor notice boards ready for the Theme Posters. In our school we have a weekly theme to encourage the whole school to concentrate efforts, prayerfully and practically, on social and personal issues. It is the RE team's task to illustrate the weekly themes for the rest of the school. This week it is my turn with reflections on homelessness. I've started something with Year 7 and we will have to finish it today. My first obstacle of the day: the desks used for the mock exams have been taken from the hall and now block the notice boards on the corridor!

So back to the staff-room and I make a start on filling in Year-9 reports. I'm actually prepared for this one as I spent an hour yesterday writing comments in my mark book. I only get five written before a bell summons me to class. It's a long step up to my room on the third floor and I arrive breathless as the 11-year-olds who reside in my room as a form base are leaving. Their cheery greetings are a Monday morning tonic. 'See you later, Mrs Richards,' calls Julia. 'See you Julia.' Yes, it's good to be here. I'm smiling when a noisy crowd of 16-year-olds push through the door ready for work.

It is break time, 10.20 a.m. and I'm shattered already. The lesson so carefully planned over the weekend never took off. I gave back the mock exam papers – which had been quite well done. This is a noisy class but they have worked well and I am confident they will be rewarded with pleasing GCSE results. But four students were missing, two of them the very ones I needed. I had directed my preparations towards them. They have missed assignments and lag behind in course work. I wanted all that completed by Christmas so that we can relax until the summer, with no written work to distract from the discussions and debates that this age group need and enjoy. We chatted about the exam paper, worked in groups to prepare the final assignment on

Christian responsibility in the Third World, and finished with a rather scattered discussion on politics and religion. I'll have to wait till next lesson to give the more ordered presentation on liberation theology that I had planned. If Sarah and Tom are still missing then – I give up!

I am slowly gathering my books together when I remember that I'm on 'break duty' today. I rush down the six flights of stairs and out into the cold grounds. I've left my anorak up in my class-room. Part-timers aren't usually called upon to do these extra duties but in our school with its scattered site we have to do our share. Notre Dame High School is an old foundation and the buildings are spread across a wide area. We need a dozen staff at a time on duty to cover all the buildings and grounds. In happier financial times teaching staff wouldn't be needed to forego break periods. So, no coffee break this morning. I return cold and somewhat wearily to the third floor, Room 48.

I like my class-room. It is a pleasant room with windows on two sides and even boasts an old sink in the corner. It started out as a biology lab and so has a huge cupboard where I can keep my teaching paraphernalia in some order. The RE staff have taken over most of this top floor in an attempt to make RE an important department in the eyes of our pupils. We've worked hard to improve on its appearance, cleaning up old desks, tidying up cupboards and painting corridor notice boards. I knew our work had not been in vain when I heard a 13-year-old boy tell a prospective parent recently, 'Here is the RE corridor. It's nice up here, our classroom is always bright and cheerful. I like RE.'

Julia and her friends arrive for my next class. They are full of good humour and I'm soon laughing again with them. We have got to get that display up on the notice boards. Four boys go downstairs and move the desks away from the display area. We check on finished posters; we put on some Christmas music and set about completing the unfinished work. The room looks a bit of a disaster when the new school governor puts his head through the door. Simon and Dominic are making a mess with the paints, a group of girls are quietly absorbed with the felt-tip pens and Claire is carefully gluing their completed works to the card. The floor is covered with paper bits and David is not making a good job of clearing it up. In the corner Emma and friends are counting out knives and forks. The visitor is intrigued and asks them what this is all about. They tell him that the school has volunteered to find two hundred china plates and cutlery for the newly formed Norwich Open Christmas charity which will provide for the Norwich homeless on Christmas Day. It has fallen to me to co-ordinate this effort.

We haven't finished when the bell rings, so there goes my dinner hour. I finish off the bits and pieces myself, Julie and Sam stay to help clear up the room and I just manage to pin up the last poster half an hour later. I grab a sandwich from the canteen and eat it whilst I pack up the last box of china plates for collection.

It is nearly one o'clock and time for a class I always enjoy. My Monday afternoon Year-10 GCSE class are a lively bunch, too big for the room – I have to bring in extra chairs. I have spent some time preparing this lesson because it completes an important section on discipleship in Mark's Gospel. I won't see the class again this term. By chance they will miss their last three lessons with me, because of a careers talk, the pantomime and a rehearsal for prize-giving. If we work hard today we can finish this topic before the holiday and start a new topic in January.

It was only as the class trooped in, with familiar faces missing that I remembered this morning's briefing. Half a dozen youngsters would be at music practices for the school concert. Once again an incomplete class which makes continuity and completion of work an impossibility. I groaned inside and reacted sharply to Martin's loud voice as he cluttered his way across the room, shouting to John to save him a place. Quick change of plan is needed. Thank God for a television in my class-room. And thank God I have a rough idea of where I want to go next with the syllabus. I look at the students, now settled, and with admirable calmness I tell them that with so many missing we will have a relaxed lesson doing background preparation for future work on conflict in Mark's Gospel. A blackboard brainstorm on 'conflict' with authority, and I'll follow with twenty minutes of *Jesus*

Christ Superstar which starts with the clash between Jesus and the Authorities. Of course it becomes obvious to the class before the end that I am not fully prepared for the discussion that follows – they are more restless than usual. What promised to be a pleasant class turns out a strain and a 'make-do'. I dash down to my afternoon break duty feeling deflated. At least I remember my anorak.

The last hour of the school day has to be better. I have my session with our large sixth-form A-level group. We team-teach this subject, Philosophy and Christian Ethics. This afternoon I will deal with the biblical background to Catholic moral teaching. Twenty-eight students in this group makes teaching in A-level style rather difficult. But I usually give the class time for discussion in groups, followed by feedback and then direct teaching.

I wasn't surprised to find plans altered once again. I hadn't anticipated the room changes The small sixth-form RE room was being used for French orals, the usually empty next-door class-room housed a drama group who had lost the hall for pantomime practice. We often use these two rooms for the discussion groups, but this afternoon we would have to make do with all the groups in the one room. It never works as well.

However the lesson went well enough except for the telephone interruption half way through. Eastern Counties Newspapers wanted an interview about the crockery and cutlery collection for Norwich Open Christmas campaign. Could they come for a photograph of all the plates stacked as high as possible? I protested that they were already packed up for delivery, but an insistent reporter persuaded me to agree. I returned to class feeling dismal at the prospect of undoing several hours' work for the sake of the press.

School finished ten minutes ago and Bert, who taught an upper-sixth class last lesson, and my two children who are in the eighth year, are pacing up and down at the school car park waiting for me to arrive. I'm in a hot fluster trying to remember what I need to take home for preparation work tonight. I grab a set of books to mark, a video to preview and a couple of files trusting, rather than checking, they are the ones I really need. I get half way down the stairs before I remember the anorak. I decide to leave it behind.

'You've had an interesting letter in the second post', says Bert, as we drive home. He tells me something about it but my mind is really on what I am going to prepare for our meal tonight. We had shepherd's pie yesterday; we seem to have had a lot of chicken lately; we can't have fish and chips again. It will have to be a pasta. I'll have to be quick to get it ready before Pedro goes for his drum lesson at the music centre.

It is eight o'clock on a Monday evening in December. I should be attending to Christmas cards, but instead I'm reading again, this time more carefully, the letter that arrived in the second post. A parent from somewhere in the South of England is deeply disturbed by an entry in one of my school textbooks. What had upset him? I search through the book to read again what I had written several years ago. The book on moral and social issues was written as background material for secondary schools, not necessarily for Catholic or church schools. This father is upset that I introduced Mary and the Virgin Birth into a discussion on the problems of infertility and surrogacy. (One of the questions for discussion read as follows: ' "In the New Testament Jesus is called the Son of God, not of Joseph. Was he born of a surrogate mother?" ') As he intends to 'take the matter to higher authority' I had better write to him. This is the gist of my argument.

> Thank you for your letter sent to me by the publisher of *Issues, What Christians Think*. As an RE teacher I'm delighted to hear of a parent helping his son with his homework. As a parent (who also helps her son with his homework) I'm only too aware of the puzzling questions we both have to tackle.
>
> I'm sorry that my book has disturbed you. Perhaps you are unaware that the question which troubles you on page 26 is a quotation. The students are asked to comment on it. Your son could make a good case in disagreeing with it on the grounds you suggest. You may be interested to know

that the quote was actually taken from a letter published in a Catholic weekly.

You may also be unaware that handbooks of GCSE material are required to be presented in an objectively neutral and non-denominational way. After all these books are offered to all schools in preparation for a GCSE exam which is open to all. Even for Catholic students, anything more slanted is likely to alienate them. It is up to the teacher, family, parish and school ethos to add their own comment.

Your son's RE teacher will presumably want to give a Roman Catholic comment on the dignity of the Mother of Christ. As a writer all I can do is to provoke discussion. It is up to your son's teacher to handle the material in a way which reflects their Catholic faith.

Most RE teachers today have an unenviable task. They have to present material to a class of students whose beliefs will range from the atheistic to the most conservative. If the teacher is not to exclude anyone (s)he has to keep discussion open and pupils interested, and remain aware of parents like you. I say this with respect – we have a duty as RE teachers to all our parents. But in order to do so we need your support, not your criticism. Some parents want traditional dogmatic teaching. Others are desperate for a very different approach. Whatever we do, we become targets for attack. I'm sure you can understand this. I hope you will show this letter to your son's teacher and discuss it.

I hope your son is enjoying the RE course and wish him all the best for the examination.

Feeling better for having cleared that letter from my desk I can settle down to an hour's preparation for tomorrow's classes.

I have introduced my pilgrimage as an RE teacher by describing this typical day. It is completely true to the education scene of the 1990s. This year I shall have my fifty-fifth birthday and so can look back over thirty years of teaching. These years have seen enormous changes in both religious and secular education.

My journey has not been without frustration and tears, but, as for most teachers I know, it has been sparked by the generosity of colleagues and above all by the good humour, common sense and honesty of the young people I love to be with.

1

MAKING A NEW START

Jesus comes to his friends
when they go under water to share Jesus' death,
and come out from it to begin a new life.[1]

We had a baptism in my class last week. Well, not a real one of course. Rebecca Jane was my daughter's once-cherished doll. Dominic, aged 12, agreed to be the father, and Gayle was game enough to offer to be mother. We chose godparents, grand-parents, aunts and uncles, and we arranged the desks to resemble a church. I asked the children if they objected to a woman priest. No problem; they agreed that it would be most appropriate for me to take on that role. They called me the Reverend Richards.

Our celebration was a happy one. There was such laughter and, to my delight, some fine moments of deep quiet when the young congregation listened to the words of the service and followed my sermon. I discovered from their homework write-up that they had all taken the lesson seriously and remembered the key points and understood the symbolism. For it was symbolism that I had in mind when I prepared the lesson.

They understood the significance of the candle, the white robe, the oils and the pouring of water. In last week's lesson we had taken a good look at water. Water giving life and water bringing death. Life-giving water for the thirsty and the filthy and for drooping flowers; death-bringing water for capsized sailors, for flooded homes and for the swimmer in rough seas.

I hope Dominic, Gayle and all their friends will remember for the rest of their lives that in their baptism they touched both meanings of water, life and death. I hope they will remember that Jesus was 'drowned' in suffering and death, and I hope they want to walk that path with him, in order to be rescued by God to live a new life.

Teaching Religious Studies day in and day out can be a great strain, for it is a constant reminder of the way I should be leading my own life. Maths or science teachers don't have the same experience. They educate their pupils to practical skills, to new fields of knowledge or to interesting facts. They can remain quite neutral about the material they teach. The RE teacher cannot. In the middle of my 'sermon' to my baptism class-congregation, I felt a pang of guilt at talking so eloquently about dying with Christ in order to rise to new life with him. I'm not at all good at it.

One boy in the class asked the inevitable question, 'Why were we baptized as babies? We didn't have any choice in the matter did we?' My usual reply seemed to satisfy him: 'One important aspect of baptism is your parents' need to celebrate your new life. They are so happy and grateful to God for this best of all gifts and they need a birthday party. Christian parents can't imagine leaving you outside the community that they find the most life-giving and precious. When my nephew was born my mother immediately knitted him a Tottenham Hotspurs hat and scarf as he was born into a football fanatic family. There was no hesitation about introducing a baby into the White Hart Lane community. At the same time they introduced him into the Christian community. Parents are like that.' The football example usually makes the point. (Mind you, the magnificent and moving sight of an adult total immersion ceremony, or the sight of a pilgrim group of Pentecostal adults commemorating their baptism in the River Jordan, is enough to make me take the children's complaint seriously. Should infants monopolize baptism so totally?)

I don't think my mother knitted me a football scarf when I was born, but she could have done since I am as fanatic a fan as anyone in the family. But she did introduce me to the Catholic community from the start. It was my mother, not my father, who had to do this because I was a child of a mixed marriage, and that meant that he had little to say in the matter. Mixed marriages were frowned upon and the Catholic Church had fixed rules about them. My mother had to seek special permission to marry my nominally Church of England father. He had to promise to bring up the children as Roman Catholics, since it is only they who have the 'fullness of the faith'. It was expected of my mother to try and persuade him to join the fold at some later time. Years later she told me that she made a mental reservation on that one, since she knew in her bones it was really an insult to my father's integrity to presume that she was in a position to force her beliefs on him. She made the decision to live her Catholic life simply and faithfully and to leave the rest to God. She died last year having fulfilled her personal decision with utmost fidelity. She was helped by my father to practise her faith, and she was encouraged by him to bring us three children up as Catholics, because my father would never dream of breaking his word. Yet he has never become a Catholic himself.

It was he who made sure my busy mother got out to Sunday Mass on time. I can hear him calling out to her, 'You've only got ten minutes to get to church; put that tea-towel down, I'll clear up. Go on. You'll be late.' I remember the pain we went through as a family when none of us three children gained the precious scholarships to the Catholic schools. It was my father who insisted that the promise he had made to educate us in the Catholic faith be kept, and that meant finding the fees to pay for our education. It even meant, in my case, refusing the scholarship I was awarded to the local County School. I stayed on at the convent and my parents sacrificed and suffered to pay for the privilege. (Eventually sympathetic school governers waived one fee to help us out.)

I am only now aware of the cost to my parents of their mixed marriage, and the profound effect this has had on my understanding of Christianity. I always took for granted my Catholic upbringing, never realizing until now that there is a world of difference between a Catholic born into a totally Catholic family and a Catholic born of a mixed marriage. I have come to understand this only recently.

My mother died suddenly, unexpectedly, one year ago (to the day) as I write. She went for a short walk around the block whilst my dad had his usual afternoon nap, and she never returned, having collapsed on the path. We'll never know how long she lay there or whether she died instantly. I didn't know she was dead when I leapt into the car following the neighbour's phone-call, so on the two-hour drive to Hertfordshire I listened to the football reports on the car radio, remembering the scores to share with her in her hospital bed. I was met at the hospital with the news of her death. Who knows which is more painful, watching a parent suffering a slow, drawn-out death, or the shock of a sudden parting with no goodbyes?

The past year has been an agony for my father as he suffers the pain of bereavement in his own silent world. His health was failing before my mother died and a year later he hangs on stubbornly to life, and we find it hard to reach to him in words beyond the superficial. It would have been very different if my mother had been left on her own, as with her I had a religious language to express belief and understanding.

I don't want to give the impression that I had or have no communication whatsoever with my father. Although he has always been the silent one, there is a sense in which I am very close to him, because we have both loved sport and shared it together. I went to Barnet football matches with him for years, and he came with me on occasions to White City Athletics and to Lords cricket ground to see England play. He encouraged me by his quiet interest when I played netball or tennis for my school. In fact we could sit for hours watching sport, never needing to speak much, but enjoying one another's company.

But it was with my mother that I explored my ideas about life and my faith in God. We never stopped talking and to the last week of her life we still laughingly 'argued' about the way to put the world right. Over the years we begged to differ in our politics and interpretation of some moral religious values, but this never mattered. In our faith, expressed in Catholic ways, we felt on firm, unshifting ground, and I could understand her love of the rosary whilst finding it of little help to me. She didn't agree with some of my more liberal Catholic ideas, but she had deepest respect for my right to have these opinions. She had a quick mind and even in her eighties she had a readiness to learn and shift positions. Her death is a grief that weighs very heavily, and has caught me rather by surprise.

A kindly nurse at the hospital advised us of the grief process, preparing us for the twists and turns of emotion that death can bring. One characteristic of bereavement, it seems, is anger: anger at sudden death, usually directed at the departed loved one for causing the pain of such a loss. I haven't felt any anger at my mother's death, only profound sadness for all the unsaid words, and a deep regret that I hadn't seen more of her in the last months of her life. I wonder if people who feel anger experience a sense of guilt later on when their emotions change again. Do they feel guilty that they felt angry? I ask this because I feel a slight sense of guilt at the judgement I am now making over my mother's decision never to talk to my father about his beliefs. I admire her gentleness and her generosity to allow others to be, but I can't help feeling now that with the best possible motives it led her to exclude my father from our Christian – Catholic – lives. For fifty-seven years of family life he was really an outsider to a vital part of it, and perhaps he was only waiting for an invitation to join in? It's an 'if only . . . time' for me now – if only we had talked more openly to Dad and asked him what he really believed. If only Mum had invited him to a celebration now and again.

I am feeling guilty because I am blaming her for his silence and his inability to express his feelings; and yet I am just as much to blame. I visit him regularly and we hardly talk for I haven't a language to reach his grief. If he had died first I know it would be different with my mother, since she would be comforted by her rosary meditations on Christ's passion and death and she would be looking forward to resurrection. I think I feel ashamed that I have no idea what my father believes. I know him enough to realize that it is too late now to change his pattern of a lifetime of ninety years, and anyway if I started to talk of God to him now I would betray my mother's resolve to put no pressure on him to conform to our way.

I have reached a paradoxical position on my pilgrimage, which has led me to discover a new tension in myself. On the one hand I staunchly uphold the ecumenical position of calling myself a Christian, not a Catholic, since this allows me to include my father in my faith community (although he is no more a Church of England member than he is a Catholic one).

On the other hand it is only this year that I have come to appreciate the Catholic Church's severe reservations on mixed marriages. In the past Catholicism has always claimed to be the true faith, and it is this that motivates the stringent discipline about mixed marriages. I appreciate the hesitation, but for a different reason. I am appalled now at the human cost of isolating one partner from a believing community.

I remember when I was only 10 years old coming to a deep conviction about God that was totally against my Catholic upbringing in school and church. Sr Mary Colomba asked me if I prayed every night to save my father's soul. I looked at her in amazement, wondering how a nun, a person supposed to be close to God, could not know the same God that I knew. My God loved my father who was the most honest, just, hard-working person you could imagine. It was unthinkable that my hero could be damned for all eternity to a separation from God and from us. From that time I have never had the slightest hesitation in accepting other Christians, or non-Christians for that matter, as fellow travellers along the road to ultimate truth. Sr Mary Colomba saw the Catholic baptism label as the single, necessary passport to heaven. I have never, ever, shared her view.

But this doesn't stop me, now, wistfully wondering what it would have been like to have shared the same faith commitment with both parents. At the very least I could rest assured that my naturally reserved, silent father was receiving an inner comfort from his knowledge of Christ's death and resurrection.

But I have learnt a further lesson on this matter from a colleague on the RE staff at my school. Chris has a very different experience of family faith from mine, since he is a son of a larger family of sons born to staunch Catholic parents. Recently, at a sixth-form conference day, I was amazed and startled to hear him bravely bare his soul to our young students. In an impassioned intervention during the discussion, he spoke about his terrible sense of loss of his traditional, family-based Catholicism.

I know Chris as a strict, no-nonsense teacher who demands high standards of his students. They respect him deeply and appreciate how he tempers his severity with them by his passionate love for Manchester United. As an intelligent, well-read Catholic, Chris is in no doubt about the need for changes in the Catholic Church, and in the way teachers present the Church to young people. I was always surprised, therefore, that Chris disliked the way some of us preferred to speak of our school as a Christian rather than a Catholic school.

I understood him for the first time when he unburdened his sense of loss to our sixth-form students. He told them how he mourned the loss of his secure Catholic upbringing. As a youth he had known exactly where he was with his Church, his school, and above all with both parents. His home life, rock solid in belief and moral standards, had been fed by attendance at Mass and benediction, at the celebration of feast days and fast days, and the recitation of October rosaries. He was looking at the young people of today, so casual in their attitude to church-going, so argumentative about their rights to live as they want, with no religious discipline as guidance, and he grieved for the old values. 'What', he said, 'do I tell my young son about Catholic values?'

I see now why Chris needs to call himself a Catholic, not a Christian. To do otherwise would be a disloyalty to his parents, and would diminish the worth of their sincere and united vision in bringing up their family. Chris is mourning, not so much the loss of Catholic identity, as the loss of childhood securities and values which form us into who we are.

I really understand now that Chris needs to call his baptism label a Catholic one and I need to call my baptism label a Christian one. Fine. We can agree to differ, just as we do over

Manchester United and Tottenham! But it isn't as easy as that, since we both teach in the same RE department and need to have some measure of uniformity in our presentation of the Church to our pupils. Yet when it comes down to it, teachers will only succeed by being absolutely true to themselves. Some sixth-formers may have winced at Chris's cry for a return to old ways, but all of them will probably remember, and be moved by, his honesty and willingness to share his pain with them. They will think seriously about what he said.

The general cry from young people at our school is for a removal of Christian barriers. They have grown up in a global world, where the animosity between religious groups stands out as a reason (or excuse) for not taking religion all that seriously. And who can blame them? The behaviour of Orthodox Christians, Catholic Christians and the Muslims in the former Yugoslavia gives enough ammunition to our young people for their claim that all denominational membership is a burden, a problem and a disaster. They certainly have a point.

I remember some years ago when I became godmother for the second time. My young nephew was baptized in a shared church in Hertfordshire. Our Roman Catholic baptism ceremony was followed by an Anglican one. As the Anglican priest and his congregation moved into the church for their christening service, there were friendly greetings on both sides but I was bemused at this strange unshared sharing. How close were we really when in the tabernacle behind the altar was a glass partition to separate the reserved eucharistic sacrament – Anglican and Catholic? A friend of ours said that a notice should be placed on the partition saying, 'In case of unity please break glass'.

My nephew and godson is now 12 years old and he attends a fine Catholic secondary school. But the pain of division has raised its ugly head again because my brother is also in a mixed marriage. He and his wife adopted a custom allowed by the Eastern Churches where one child follows the religion of the father, one of the mother. My sister-in-law wanted the second son to wait for baptism until he was older, and my brother respected her view. It seemed likely that the time was near for baptism just as he was ready to transfer to secondary school. He wanted to go to his brother's school, and being in a Christian school would be the best background for receiving baptism anyway. We all presumed that he would have no problem in getting a place, with his older brother doing so well and parents who supported the school wholeheartedly. Unfortunately his parents decided to be absolutely honest and not push the baptism through just to 'make sure of his place'. They didn't go in for such dishonesty. It is clear now that they should have 'played the game', because the unbaptized lad has been refused a place at the school. Friends' and acquaintances' children will be going there, some of whom never go near a church, and some of whom admit they only applied because the school has a good educational standard.

I am appalled that the governors/selection committee who decided to turn my young nephew away still see baptism as a kind of mystical formula which marks out the saved from the lost. How insensitive and blind is the decision to tell an 11-year-old, 'We don't want you here but we don't mind having your brother because he is part of the Christian community and you are not.' I am amazed that they don't seem to be aware of the harm they have done to that family by creating tension and division. They have shut the door on a young boy who, after all, had no say about his baptism. My sister-in-law's opinion has been rubbished, and she has a right to feel angry and alienated. The one certain thing is that whoever turned her son away has absolutely no understanding of the dynamic of family life. I have to suspect the priest/governor who would, after all, never know the delicate task of parents in building up the confidence of a second child who lives in the shadow of a bright, successful elder brother.

Many years ago I attended a lecture in Oxford given by a Russian Orthodox scholar, Nicholas Zernov. He presented most eloquently his thesis that Christ would be utterly ashamed of his followers for putting so many man-made obstacles in the way of unity. 'I want', he said, 'a passport for my journey towards God. But the passport I want is a dual one, one which allows me to belong to more than one country.' He described those countries as the Christian denominations. Most of the time he lived and felt comfortable in one (Orthodox) country, but at times he wanted a change. He wanted to feel free to enter another country. But we don't issue passports like that, only embargos and restrictions. We keep people out and we don't welcome people in, not unless they intend to abandon their own country for good. I have always wholeheartedly agreed with Nicholas Zernov that we were baptized into Christ, not into denominations.

> For as many of you as were baptised into Christ have put on Christ. There is neither Jew nor Greek, there is neither male nor female; for you are all one in Christ Jesus.
>
> (Galatians 3:27–28, RSV)

If Paul were writing today, wouldn't he add, 'There is neither Methodist, nor Anglican, nor Roman Catholic, there is neither Baptist nor United Reformed; for you are all one in Christ Jesus'?

If my second experience of godparenting made me raise my eyebrows, the first experience was even more puzzling. My best friend at school, Barbara, decided to become a Catholic. We wanted to go to college together but as an Anglican she could not attend the Catholic teacher-training college that had accepted me. We remained close friends and on her twenty-first birthday, with the reluctant resignation of her parents, she was 'received into the Church'. I was surprised that the priest seemed to be baptizing her all over again. I had presumed her Anglican baptism had brought her to Christ already. She was certainly the most serious Christian I knew, and her life of prayer put me to shame. Today Barbara is a Carmelite nun. I will always insist that she learnt to love God and come close to him at her parents' knee and from their example, as much as from the Catholic influence of our convent school. I don't know what her 'Catholic' baptism meant.

Bert, my husband, was having the same reservations at about the same time, when a former Anglican priest joined the staff of St Edmund's College where he was teaching. Patrick and his wife and children were preparing to become Catholics. He was aghast to discover that they were expected to be re-baptized. He flatly refused, especially since he had baptized his own children as an Anglican priest. How could he accept the implication that it had all been invalid? He finally made his point, and the pressure for re-baptism was removed. He had wryly pointed out that the only reason he intended to become 'Roman Catholic' was because he believed he had, in fact, been baptized into the Church anyway.

When my own children were adopted we had another strange baptism experience. Pedro and Blanca already had our Catholic background because they were born in Colombia, South America. The poverty of their beginning resulted in the odd situation of one twin (destined for survival) being baptized at birth and one not. The lovely, warm-hearted, elderly priest who welcomed us as a family decided to baptize both of them 'just in case'. In case what? Bert once wrote of this mentality:

> We have all come across people who have their children baptised in much the same way as they might have them vaccinated. 'Better be on the safe side', or 'It can't do them any harm.' And to judge by the Sunday afternoon goings on in some parishes, there are priests who don't rate it as highly as vaccination. It is a ritual to be got through, and there's no point in being too fussy about details. After all, it's performed on an unconscious infant, and it works *ex opere operato.*

But I didn't complain at the attitude which resulted in the twins' baptism, because it proved to be such a happy occasion. the babies were baptized (or re-baptized) in the school hall at Notre Dame where I had been teaching. This time my class had two real babies to baptize, not dolls, and we sang and we celebrated and we laughed and we welcomed the two of them into the community. I remember most of all the hearty singing of the hymn of St Francis that praised God for the gift of creation.

Laudato sii, o mi Signore.
Praise to you for little children,

brother Pedro, sister Blanca,
Praise to you most Holy Spirit,
life and joy of all creation.

Laudato sii, o mi Signore.
For our life is but a song
and the reason for our singing
is to praise you for the music,
join the dance of your creation.[2]

That is how I want to see baptism celebrated. It isn't a mumbo-jumbo of magic words that ensures the baby's soul is rescued from a state of original sin. The grizzly old teaching told us that babies who die can't go to heaven, and so are relocated in limbo, because they are not in a state of redeemed grace. This seems to have disappeared from the textbooks. Thank goodness.

I see baptism as the joyful celebration of life, by a Christian community announcing to the world that every child is a child of God. And when parents suffer the unspeakable agony of losing a baby, I would want to assure them that their son or daughter has died out of original sin, that is to say, out of the struggling, messed-up world we have made, and into the love of God. The only limbo is the lonely, broken heart of a bereaved parent.

Resolutions for the class-room

Writing about baptism into Christ has been a chance to meditate and pray about the meaning of this sacrament, which marks the beginning of my pilgrimage of faith. As a teacher called to share my vision of Christian life with young people I need to decide what is appropriate to say and do in the class-room. I can't share everything with the students. They need a clear, positive, cheerful presentation. Three practical ideas have emerged which seem to sum up the ideas I would want to explore with them.

First idea

In the Church of Saint Sulpice in Paris (some years ago) the baptistry was carefully and colourfully designed to instruct visitors on the meaning of baptism. A number of large panels displayed magnificent photographs and captions showing the powerful symbolism of the ceremony. Next time I teach this unit I won't only have a class baptism, but I will also create a wonderful baptistry, and the children can work in groups to make the panels.

Panel 1

Pictures of athletes being massaged with oil, and oil being added to food in cooking. Pictures of salt being reclaimed from salt marshes, and salt being rubbed into meat.
'May he strengthen you with his power.'
'Receive the salt of wisdom.'

Panel 2

Pictures of water: the tide washing up on a littered beach, fish in water, waterfalls, watering the garden. Surf-riders buried in water.
'You have been buried with Christ in his death and with him risen to a new life.'

Panel 3

Baptism in the River Jordan. Jesus' baptism in the Jordan. Adult baptisms in the Jordan today. Collage of faces, young and old, all nationalities.
'I will be to them a Father and they shall be my sons and daughters.'

Panel 4

Pictures of misery, bombings, deforestation. Newspaper headlines of tragedy and horror. In the middle a large cross.
'No one can serve two masters; you cannot serve God and money.'
'Go then, marked with the sign of the cross.'

Panel 5
Pictures of light: sunlight, moonlight, candles and, by contrast, darkness, fog.
'He who follows me walks not in darkness.'

Panel 6
Pictures of churches, pilgrimages, crowds of people, open doors.
'I will be their God and they will be my People.'

If we can produce a really good display, perhaps the local clergy may like to use it in church at their baptism ceremonies.

Second idea
Giving a name at baptism is an important part of the symbolism. It is a fun lesson to explore the meanings of the children's names. My 'Naming Baby' book is well thumbed already. It is a good time to talk about the uniqueness of each person – each one made in God's image but each one special and chosen. Taking our fingerprints and comparing them is a cheerful start to this lesson. Gerard Markland's hymn, based on words from Isaiah, can become a theme song for our lessons.

Do not be afraid,
for I have redeemed you.
I have called you by your name;
you are mine.

1. When you walk through the waters, I'll be with you.
   You will never sink beneath the waves.
2. When the fire is burning all around you,
   you will never be consumed by the flames.
3. When the fear of loneliness is looming,
   then remember I am at your side.
4. When you dwell in the exile of the stranger,
   remember you are precious in my eyes.
5. You are mine, O my child; I am your father,
   and I love you with a perfect love.[3]

Then on a similar theme I would like to explore with a group of older pupils a text of St Paul, written to the church at Philippi whilst he was in prison. It is a wonderful letter with a strong emphasis on the love and unity which should characterize the Christian community. He urges his friends to stop squabbling because it destroys in them the image of Christ. Paul tells the Philippians that they must face life as Jesus did:

> Like Adam, he was the image of God;
> but unlike Adam, did not presume
> that being like God meant to domineer.
>
> He knew it meant to renounce all claims,
> except the claim to be servant of all.
>
> So he lived the life of a human being,
> and accepted the human fate, which is death,
> even the shameful death of a slave.
> That is why God has raised him up,
> and given him a name beyond compare:
>
> Every creature, living and dead,
> will kneel to him, and give glory to God,
> and echo the cry, 'Jesus is Lord'.
>
> (Philippians 2:5–11, tr. H. J. Richards)

Paul sees in Jesus, as in an undistorting mirror, what God is really like. In Jesus he can understand the God who is otherwise a total mystery. That is why Jesus can be given the name which the Jewish Scriptures (Old Testament) reserve for God himself, Kyrios or Lord. Jesus reveals the whole meaning of the word God, and at the same time the whole meaning of the word man.

The wonder of baptism is that we receive not only our unique, chosen name, but we recognize (our family recognize on our behalf) that we are, like Christ, made in the image of God. When a new mother gazes into the face of her baby she can glimpse the awesome mystery of God. That is what we celebrate.

Third idea

In my reading recently I came again upon an incident from our European history which I would like to share with older students. Paul Tillich tells the following story:

> In the Nuremberg war-crime trials a witness appeared who had lived for a time in a grave in a Jewish graveyard, in Wilna, Poland. It was the only place he – and many others – could live, when in hiding, after they had escaped the gas chamber. During this time he wrote poetry, and one of the poems was a description of a birth. In a grave near by, a young woman gave birth to a boy. The eighty-year-old gravedigger, wrapped in a linen shroud, assisted. When the newborn child uttered his first cry, the old man prayed: 'Great God, hast thou finally sent the Messiah to us? For who else than the Messiah himself can be born in a grave?'[4]

What a starting-point for a quiet class reflection on Christ the Messiah, the one who was born in the grave! We could spend time looking at the poetry of the psalms and the wise insight of Paul into the mystery of Christ, 'the first-born from the dead'.

> Save me, O God!
> I am in deep water,
> and the waves are about to drown me . . .
> Don't let the flood come over me;
> don't let me drown in the depths
> or sink into the grave.
>
> (*Psalm 69*)

How often the weary pilgrim feels like this; waters threaten to flood over her, or the rock he once felt beneath his feet turns to shifting sand. No need for despair for

> Jesus comes to his friends
> when they go under water to share Jesus' death
> and come out from it to begin a new life.

2

FEED THE WORLD

> Jesus comes to his friends
> when they break bread and pour wine for
> each other, and so remember his broken body
> and the blood he poured out on the cross.

Every Friday morning at school we have an optional school Mass, during the time set aside for pastoral work. Last week I was greatly distracted because I had this chapter of the book on my mind. I looked around at the seventy pupils, a good mix of boys and girls and fairly representative of all age groups. A handful of teachers, not committed to form duties, also attended. Our pupils come from many different parts of Norfolk and Suffolk and priests from across these counties come in turn to celebrate with us.

Fr Michael took as his theme of the Mass the idea of the Christian community meeting as friends and expressing their friendship in shared communion. He started his preaching with a negative: 'We are meeting as friends, but if you look around I expect you know very little about each other. You are acquainted but hardly friends.' I wondered how he would get out of such a poor start. He didn't really. He only stumbled on, telling us that by coming to Mass and communion we were meeting Jesus our friend. By being close to him we were, in fact, friends with each other. I could see what he was trying to say but I'm not sure the message got across. Don't get me wrong; I'm not criticizing Fr Michael. I share his perplexity in trying to convey to others what it is about the sacrament of Eucharist that makes us call it the heart of Christian community and the centre of Christian worship.

I got up early today to start writing this chapter – then I did some ironing, fed the cat (again), washed up odds and ends, walked around the house looking for another distraction, and now armed with my third coffee am reluctantly at the word processor. Reluctant because I hardly know where to begin. For me, the Eucharist is both at the heart of my faith and the cause of my deepest worry about teaching doctrine. If the ARCIC group (Anglican-Roman Catholic International Commission) met for a span of several years to discuss the meaning of this central doctrine of faith, and can come to no very clear conclusion, it is hardly surprising that we teachers find it difficult to talk about it to our pupils. The problem is most graphically expressed in the press reports of the film *Alive*, the story of the Andean plane crash where survivors resorted to eating their dead comrades. One review said, 'Many have pointed to the Catholic symbolism inherent in the tale down to the Eucharistic eating of flesh.'

This association with cannibalism is just one question that comes up in any discussion on the Eucharist. There are many other questions too, and none of them are easy for the teacher to handle. What really happened at the Last Supper? What *is* transubstantiation? Why no inter-communion between Christians? How is Christ present in the Eucharist? To whom does the Eucharist 'belong'? What kind of liturgy is appropriate for the celebration of Eucharist? Where does 'feeding the world' fit in?

I ask this last question with agony as I look at a small holy picture which I bought in the church shop yesterday. A gold chalice of wine, the white hosts on a gold paten and a beautiful crystal vase of spring flowers all standing on a red silk background, with the words 'Our God feeds the hungry to their heart's content' (Psalm 107). What does this rich symbolism say to the starving children of the Sudan whose gaunt pictures stare out of my Sunday Supplement?

Let me start searching for answers to some of these questions in the gospel. What really happened at the Last Supper and on Calvary? When I was a secondary-school pupil, forty years ago, the answer to that question was clear, unequivocal and not to be questioned. After all, I learnt the catechism by heart in RE lessons. I can recite No. 277 now:

> *What is the Holy Mass?*
> The Holy Mass is the Sacrifice of the Body and Blood of Jesus Christ, really present on the altar under the appearances of bread and wine, and offered to God for the living and the dead.[1]

(I remember that I didn't learn the questions that followed this one for homework, so I was forbidden to play in a dinner-hour netball match for my House. It is the only occasion I can recall when I deliberately defied school authority. I ignored Sister Imelda's detention and played my match.)

For good or ill we don't get children to learn much by heart these days. We try instead to get them involved. My class for the 12-year-olds on the Eucharist this term took the form of a *seder* (Passover) meal. I simplified the order of service that my husband has produced in booklet form (Hubert Richards, *The Passover Meal*, McCrimmons 1990). As classes go this was a high success. We sat in rearranged desks around the room, and I outlined the meaning of Passover for the Jewish people. The class knew the Exodus story as they had already produced newspaper reports on the event for the 'Hebrew Herald', with eye-catching headlines like, 'The Pharaohgate Affair' and 'Moses Leads a Getaway'. I was keen to point out that the Jews really do invite non-Jewish outsiders to share this experience of liberation with them. A rubric actually says, 'Let all who are hungry come and eat; let all who are in need come and share our Passover.'

We followed the celebration rubrics, lighting the candles, drinking Ribena and saying grace; four children had prepared the questions, I had arranged the baskets of mazza bread, parsley, salt water, horseradish as bitter herbs, and mini-Easter eggs as the sweet. I had to pretend my bone was a lamb bone. We sang *Go Down Moses* accompanied by Louis Armstrong on an LP, and two boisterous boys searched for Elijah in the corridor. They brought back a teacher who happened to be passing and we decided she wasn't Elijah but she joined in anyway.

It was a good occasion and led naturally into a study of the Gospel texts for Holy Week. I realize now how I have shifted the emphasis of my teaching on the Eucharist over the years. Then I took my lead from those catechism questions. Today I explore the Jewishness of Jesus and we try to understand how he felt at the Last Supper. We look at the Pauline and Gospel texts which describe that last meal and interpret them in the light of the Jewish conviction that the Passover event of 1250 BC in Egypt is actually present in the lives of those who celebrate the memory of the original occasion.

It is in this way I emphasize the continuing presence of Jesus in the Eucharist. At the Last Supper he indicated that his love for all people had reached its fulfilment. Seeing the inevitability of his death he said, 'This is my body given for you . . . This is my blood shed for you . . . Do this in memory of me.' In Passover language Jesus embraced his death on the cross. In that death, he made known the measure of the love of God which reaches out to everyone. With the 12-year-olds I let the class-room celebration speak for itself. I only mention that Jesus is like the Passover lamb, whose death brought about liberation.

In my early days of teaching I took pains to emphasize that Jesus' death was our salvation. I used the traditional church language accumulated over the ages by Christian thinkers. I would examine the images used to explain the doctrine of salvation. (These are the images which occur in sermons during Lent.) I used, for example, the language describing theories of *satisfaction, propitiation, sacrifice, redemption* and *atonement*. But I've discovered that few Christians today find these medieval images helpful. This is understandable as they were based on concrete, legalistic language of another age. They are not useless descriptions of course; they simply illustrate how people have struggled to speak of the God who is beyond all human thinking. But in all these images it is God who demands Jesus' death, an idea which doesn't seem to fit with Jesus' understanding of God as portrayed in the Gospels.

I wonder what people do imagine is the reality when they still sing at Easter:

> Bring, all ye dear-bought nations, bring,
> your richest praises to your king,
> alleluia, alleluia.
> That spotless Lamb, who more than due,
> *paid* for his sheep, and those sheep you,
> Alleluia.
> That guiltless Son, who *bought* your peace,
> and made his Father's *anger* cease,
> alleluia, alleluia.
> O thou, whose power o'ercame the grave,
> by grace and love us sinners *save*
> Alleluia.[2]

There is, of course, little of this kind of commercial language in the New Testament. The Gospel authors turn more easily to the image of 'revelation'. Jesus reveals a new understanding of God. He embodied Godliness in a human life. Where people had thought of God as distant and judgemental, Jesus portrayed God as being close, compassionate, forgiving and liberating. Nowhere was this seen more clearly than in the life of Jesus himself, and nowhere was this more evident than in his acceptance of death, without hitting back. It wasn't God who demanded death, it was sinful men. But God forgives them even for killing his son. Christians believe that this understanding of God, when accepted, changes everything. It frees people from their burdens, it brings them close to a loving God, it inspires them in turn to be compassionate, forgiving and merciful. This is the liberation of Passover that we celebrate at Easter and at every Mass or communion service.

Some years ago, when I was a student at Corpus Christi College, I tried to put this understanding of the death of Jesus into a poem. I wrote it on the underground between Tottenham Court Road and Notting Hill Gate.

Christ on the cross,
Not crushed by death,
But broken by his love too deep for knowing;
Christ on the cross,
Not crushed by death,
But living on in love too deep for crushing.

Christ on the cross
Not slain for sin
But broken by his love too great for giving;
Christ on the cross,
Not crushed by death,
But living on in love too great for slaying.

Christ on the cross,
Not killed by man,
But broken by his love too strong for holding;
Christ on the cross,
Not crushed by death,
But living on in love too strong for killing.

Theology is heady stuff. The pain of being an RE teacher lies in the problem of communicating it. Choosing words and images which will not put young people off – that is a constant challenge.

I watched the faces of one class when they were participating in a class Mass. The priest was a friend to them so they were generally interested in the liturgy and took part in it with good will. But when he lifted the host and said slowly and with enormous emphasis 'THIS IS JESUS, the Lamb of God who takes away your sins', I saw several of the 13-year-olds frown, or raise an eyebrow. The language was not helpful. I would prefer the priest to keep to the traditional language, 'Behold, the Lamb of God'. This allows for the mystery and the Passover symbolism to be appreciated. Holding out the host and saying 'This is Jesus' is not the same – it is too literal and physical.

It was even worse when I heard another priest, the celebrant in a Mass for first communicants, say 'You are going to *eat* the body of Jesus, and *drink* his blood.' Can 7-year-olds cope with such cannibalistic language?

Now I recognize that this is the language used in John's Gospel, chapter 6. But John's theology is difficult to communicate to young children; and because I won't use this language myself I know I am sometimes looked upon with suspicion by church members. Of course I believe that Jesus is present to me in the sacrament, as he is present in other ways in my life and in my experience of community. But not in such a crude way that I would describe myself as 'eating' him.

Traditionalists blame 'liberal' teachers for the decline in church attendance and the seeming indifference of young people to the sacraments. They believe that teachers are 'watering down' the faith. After years of experience and concern to share my faith with others, I can honestly say that it is not the liberalism of teachers, but the clumsy use of religious language that has prevented us communicating our faith and keeping children interested enough in the Church to stay with it until they are old enough to think for themselves about the mystery of God.

This came home to me most clearly when my own children were preparing for their first communion. I was horrified to hear Pedro say, 'Mummy, Matthew said that Fr Robin had blood in the cup. He wouldn't drink that, would he? Yuk!' Six years later, Pedro remains reluctant to receive the cup at the altar. He usually passes it by. Bert and I were further disturbed when we were regaled with a very odd bedtime story in the same week. Sometimes the children composed stories for us. This was 6-year-old Blanca's:

> Mummy what do you think of this? Supposing you turned into a biscuit or bread; no, into an apple pie? And somebody ate you up. Then you suddenly turned back into you. And that very big, enormous person you were inside, suddenly

ate a strawberry, but you were struggling to get out, so he bit your fingers or your toes.

I remember laughing with Blanca over her strange story. But we couldn't help feeling it was related to the first communion preparations. Was Blanca's peculiar story the result of a 6-year-old's vivid imagination trying to make sense of the notion of 'receiving Jesus' in communion? Whatever does a young child actually make of this talk of eating the body of Jesus in the form of bread? I told Blanca's teacher about her 'breadtime story' as we call it. She told me how difficult she finds it to talk to the children in a language that makes sense and that conveys the truth without confusion. We have been lucky because our children happen to have attended fine Catholic schools where great care has been taken in using God language. And yet Blanca and her friends still picked up cannibalistic ideas. Their teacher admitted that she herself had just been asked by one 7-year-old if communion tasted like meat, 'Because you are eating a body'.

We need to be far more concerned about what our children understand when we adults use theological, God language. Young children make the most profound statements and they offer quite logical answers to their own questions. And all too often we step in and confuse them. It seems strange to me now that we Roman Catholics prepare our children for their first communion at the very age when their imaginations are most wild and wonderful. Strange, that is, only if we insist on presenting the sacrament as 'eating the body of Jesus in communion'. This is the age when children can recite by heart the stories of Red Riding Hood and the Gingerbread Man; stories where people are gobbled up. And this is the age when they collect dinosaur models and are most captivated by the carnivores that eat the flesh of other dinosaurs. 7-year-olds will love Jurassic Park!

Bert and I decided to prepare our children for first communion by simply talking about remembering Jesus as we share bread and wine. We felt we had good Gospel backing as we concentrated on John's account of the Last Supper, where Jesus talks about loving and serving one another, with no mention of the bread 'being' or 'becoming' his body. It didn't quite solve the problem, of course, because Pedro and Blanca were already exposed to the language used at church and picked up from others at school.

I quoted these examples when I had to address a Diocesan Pastoral Conference for Laity. I was immediately taken to task for 'watering down the true doctrine of transubstantiation'. The objection didn't come from the bishop who was present, but from a group of young protesters who turned out to be Opus Dei members. What right have these guardians of 'truth' to tell me what to think, or how correctly to formulate my faith? My heart went out to those in church authority (bishops and priests, pastoral and parochial councils) who have to cope with such self-appointed 'guardians of truth'.

If those Opus Dei youngsters had been open enough, and if there had been time enough, I could have explained how parents experience the marvel of the presence of God's Spirit in their own children, before they have been assaulted by adult religious language. I would have described the Easter when my son was only six. Leaving church one Sunday he asked, 'Mummy, is Jesus really alive? 'Cos if he is, why haven't we asked him round to our house?' And with a customary chuckle, he added, 'and I think I would give him a cheese sandwich'. Pedro's response to an 'alive' Jesus was the most Christian one I could wish for him – biblical, in fact. He would invite him in and offer him food. His Easter understanding was the Emmaus story. As a Christian parent I see it as far more important that my son understands the heart of the gospel than that he can use theological jargon accurately (that is, as a medieval thinker formulated it).

I would also have wanted to tell the Opus Dei group that my son had understood the heart of the Emmaus story because it corresponded to his own gentle, generous self. Teachers have long known that the best learning is that which builds on what is already felt and experienced. You start where the children are at, was the frequent refrain in my college years. Pedro's response to an 'alive' Jesus was his normal welcoming response to others. That's how he is. I remember when the children went to their first play group. I took the opportunity to do some writing whilst I waited for them. From my room I could watch the children unnoticed when they went to the outdoor play area. There was a very difficult boy in the group, a highly disturbed youngster whose behaviour was destructive and negative. I watched him one day playing, as usual, alone in the sand pit. Suddenly Pedro approached him, slowly. He sat near him; he moved closer; he offered him a toy truck. I watched with bated breath as the boy snatched it away. Pedro stayed there quietly and within five minutes the two of them were playing peacefully together. And I had secretly hoped that Pedro and his sister would avoid the problem children and play with the well-behaved, conforming ones.

I had reason to feel humbled because the book I was writing at that moment was a commentary on Luke's Gospel, the Gospel whose theme is the caring Jesus who accepted the outcasts and sought the company of the most despised. I knew all the Christian ideals and could speak and interpret the holy and the theological language. But 3-year-old Pedro was being the follower of Jesus. Not me.

It is experiences like these that make me want to shout from the rooftops. My experience of young people in school and my family life bring me constantly into the presence of God. I can understand the Jesus of the Gospels in the light of ordinary, everyday life. The message I want to pass on to everyone I meet can be summarized in the following way. All our religious words seem unnecessary in the presence of a human experience that is illuminated by love, acceptance, forgiveness and welcome. We are always in danger of imposing holy words on a reality which is totally human and secular. I am afraid that we can make Christian life very difficult for our children if we start putting 'holy' labels on their most human and instinctive responses. For God is present when love is present. If incarnation means anything at all it means that God is present precisely in the most secular and human events of our daily lives. Putting religious words on to the reality doesn't make it any more real. For children it can be counterproductive. It can add a magic dimension and so remove God into the area of the unreal, the fantasy world.

Many of my older pupils dismissed the church God from their lives when they recognized the unreality of their fantasy world of childhood. My task as a secondary teacher is to reinstate their God.

The Opus Dei group are not the only ones who had difficulty with my ideas about inappropriate religious language for young children. At about the same time I was asked to write a contribution by the editor of a well-known Catholic journal. I spent some hours preparing my article and was happy with the result. He wasn't. I was surprised by this because he accepts articles which reveal gross injustices in the Church or which are openly critical of the Pope. But he could not accept my article on the grounds that it touched upon the sacred words of doctrinal language which cannot be questioned. He wrote:

> Perhaps I could refer to the thing that caused me most uneasiness. You say that 'We have decided to prepare our children for communion by simply talking about remembering Jesus when we share bread and wine.' But surely that is to impose as adults on your children? Why tell them something which is only part of the truth, and which in Catholic eyes risks obscuring the truth? Are not children defended against danger precisely because of the fantasy world which they naturally inhabit at that time?

On reading this again I still remain astonished at the logic. I can only suppose the editor had no children of his own. I replied at the time:

> In answer to your first question, 'Why tell children only part of the truth?' Because that is the only part of the truth they can grasp at this age. Do we have to tell them everything at the age of six? Including transubstantiation, the two natures of Chalcedon, and papal infallibility?

I could, of course, have added that no one suggests we tell 6-year-olds everything about sexual relationships. He would surely have accepted that parents and others answer children's questions about sex honestly and openly only when they are ready for it. We wouldn't tell infants about the Church's teaching on sexual intercourse within marriage or on the use of contraceptives. That comes much later. Perhaps my editor came from a good Jesuit background that claims 'Give me a child until he is seven . . . '.

The Jesuit phrase is not untrue: psychologists point out that the earliest years of life are the most impressionable. If a child is loved and respected in those early years she has the best possible start in life. If a child is ignored or abused his life is most likely to be damaged. I question whether indoctrination is a form of abuse.

With this chapter in mind I sat down recently with a group of 14-year-olds to talk about celebrating the Eucharist. I wanted to listen to their ideas and problems. The almost unanimous cry was not unexpected: 'Going to Mass is totally boring and it doesn't speak to our age group at all.' I relayed this message to the parish AGM when the question of youth interest (or lack of it) came up. I noticed one lady in front of me vigorously shake her head in disagreement. Her 13-year-old son is very interested in church – he is a leading altar server – and the whole family are 100 per cent plus involved in the parish. Her point was taken up by the priest in charge of altar boys, who told me there is no problem at all with the families and children he knew. 'Let them serve on the altar', he said, 'then they would be interested.' I took their point, firstly because family involvement is important and secondly it helps if you are a boy! 'What of the girls?' I asked and was dismissed with the answer, 'Don't go up that path. The Pope doesn't want altar girls and we don't have them here.' I have enormous sympathy with my pupils, and patronizing remarks like this make me angry and inclined to walk away from the parish. Fortunately other priests are more understanding.

I want to speak up for the 90 per cent of my pupils who as generous, open young people are willing to listen for God's voice in their lives. They genuinely are unable to find such relevance in the Church as it appears to them. (The other 10 per cent are regular church-goers.) I find it sad that 'good' church attending adults often dismiss these 90 per cent, blaming their families or teachers for not keeping them 'practising'. I find comfort in the gospel because Jesus was much more interested and sympathetic towards those who drifted to the edge. He would be sitting in my class-room with the groups who are dissatisfied with the establishment, rather than attending the 11 o'clock High Mass.

My group outlined the reasons for their lack of enthusiasm for weekly church-going. Will those in charge please listen to what they are saying!

1. The liturgy is usually long and not in a style we can identify with.
2. The whole Church is sexist and male-dominated. Girls are made to feel inferior. We want women priests.
3. Why can't we have inter-communion between denominations? No wonder Serbs fight Croats. We call on Christians to unite.
4. The bread is supposed to be Jesus. But how? All this talking of eating Jesus seems unreal and rather distasteful.

I suppose some RE teachers would find no problem in answering these criticisms along the party-line. But I have to wrestle with my own problem here because I sympathize with my pupils and share their criticisms. Yet out of loyalty to my Church, and because of the trusted position I am in, I have to search for some explanation which does not offend my community. Let me look at their four questions.

1. *Liturgical style* is a problem. people have different needs and the congregation at a parish Mass is an artificial community. It is made up of young and old, traditional and liberal thinkers, people of Mediterranean, Irish and Anglo-Saxon background. On top of this there are times when each one needs something different. Sometimes I want a quiet, meditative liturgy, but when I feel in another mood I want to sing and dance. Liturgy should be created. It is imposed on us rather than created by us. This is at the heart of the problem for teenagers. What if we could return to the early Church experience?

Say we took St Justin's description of the Eucharist (*c.* 150 AD), a short community celebration with just three parts. A *Kiss of Peace* between all the community leads into the *Eucharistic Prayer*, a thanksgiving and praise from Scripture as the bread and wine are offered. The climax is the *Communion*, generally received under both kinds and then taken out to share with absent family and friends. The simplicity of this more spontaneous, small group celebration was lost as centuries of liturgists added to and formalized the celebration. Over the centuries the sense of community disappeared as the Eucharist was described in the most exalted terms because it contained the 'divine presence of Jesus'. After St Cyril called the Mass 'that most terrifying hour' people were frightened to communicate, and the moment of consecration became a new focal point of the liturgy. People 'attended' Mass, they no longer celebrated a Eucharist. The priest, speaking in Latin, had his back to the people and he raised the host for people to adore. This is far removed from the original Passover meal of Jesus and his companions. My husband tells of the man he knew who actually thought that when the priest raised his hands above his head it was to catch the host as the 'Bread from Heaven' mysteriously appeared from God. He was very surprised when priests began to celebrate the Mass facing the congregation and he saw that the host was on the altar all the time! Amazingly that discovery did not upset his faith.

Vatican II in the 1960s made a valiant attempt to return the Eucharist to the community. It hasn't worked yet for the majority of young Christians. I would like to go back to Justin's celebration and let small communities celebrate spontaneously and in response to their own local needs. We would need a new understanding of priestly power. But that is another story in chapter 5.

2. The Church of England is at present expressing for my pupils its own problems with *sexism* in the Church. I am almost bemused that those in the Church of England who oppose women's ordination imagine a Roman Catholic Church supporting them. We are as divided as they are. I know very few Catholics who believe that priesthood must remain open only to men; and I know very many women in my church who feel distressed by discrimination.

I recognize that the Church of England argument is more to do with the authority of the General Synod, but I suspect the Catholic laity are just as divided about papal authority. I found this poem in Donald Hilton's anthology *Liturgy of Life*. It expresses everything I want to say.

> Did the woman say, as she held him for the first time,
> in the dark of the stable,
> after the pain, the bleeding and the crying,
> This is my body, this is my blood?
>
> Did the woman say, as she held him for the last time,
> in the dark of the garden,
> after the pain, the bleeding and the dying,
> This is my body, this is my blood?
>
> Well that she said it for him then,
> for dried old men,
> brocaded robes belying barrenness,
> ordain that she not say it for him now.[3]

3. Ali is one of my most enthusiastic pupils. Her faith and commitment to Christian values is outstanding. She is a practising Church of England member, the only one alongside twenty-six Catholics. At school Masses she is invited to receive a blessing, whilst many of her non church-going companions receive communion. No *inter-communion* for her. 'Why', she asks me, 'am I not allowed to receive the Lord in the school community that I love so much?' Why not indeed? I could weep for her. At communion in my parish I stand alongside Catholics who have very different interpretations of doctrine to mine. Ask any group of Christians what they understand by the eucharistic presence of Jesus and you will get an enormous variety of answers. Catholic will not necessarily agree with Catholic and Anglican will not necessarily agree with Anglican. I know Anglicans who would give the same answer as mine, or the same as my bishop's. The Council of Trent called the Eucharist 'the symbol of unity and

love'. What irony. That is what it isn't. So do we change the symbol or do we change the reality of disunion to get closer to the gospel? I have to admit to being totally impatient with authorities who try and talk first and look for theological definitions to repair our human failure in community. We could talk forever about the actual meaning of the eucharistic symbol. ARCIC I spent years on it with no result. Surely we should change first the reality of disunity by welcoming others in shared communion. One of the ARCIC signatories, Bishop Cormac Murphy O'Connor, expected a move in this direction, following the talks. He wrote in 1985 that both Churches would soon be in a position to take practical steps towards unity:

> . . . there would be agreements to share facilities for theological education; there would be joint exploration of new forms, or worship and retreats in common. There would be much interchange of preachers for the homily during the celebration of the Eucharist and a greater development with regard to Sacramental sharing.

I wonder if it worries the bishop that for ten years his admirable vision, with regard to inter-communion, has never materialized. Not in the West, that is; I am told that the problem doesn't arise for the Latin American Churches. Latin Americans don't see a problem. They raise their hands and with smiling faces say, 'We have one Lord, of course we celebrate together.'

The whole issue of inter-communion is nothing new in Europe. I saw whilst half glancing at television over Easter a medieval painting under discussion. I missed the name of the artist! It seems he had painted a liturgical scene where a community gathered around the eucharistic table. The Church rejected the painting because a bishop noticed he had painted in a number of known, non-Roman Catholics at the gathering. They only accepted the gift when the artist changed the title to the Feast at Cana, to make it an ordinary meal.

Inter-communion is obviously discussed around the world. I heard of two Australian bishops who were talking about the problem of not knowing if those who presented themselves for communion were Catholics. 'What do you do?' asked one bishop. 'I do what Jesus would have done'. 'You don't!'

Jodee, aged twelve, showed great wisdom and theological insight I thought when she commented to me at our class Passover meal, 'How come the churches won't have intercommunion if the Mass is our Passover meal and you said that Jews are happy to invite non-Jewish outsiders to share the experience with them? Jesus was a Jew so he welcomed outsiders. We keep them out.'

4. The doctrine of the *Real Presence* is at the heart of the problem. Volumes and volumes are written on it. Most are so difficult to follow that what the writer is saying is totally unintelligible to most of us. I don't find Herbert McCabe OP as difficult as some philosophers/theologians. But I have just read, re-read and re-read an article on Real Presence that he wrote some years ago. I hung on for most of it especially in the interesting contrast between empiricist and post-empiricist philosophy. The empiricist says that a word has meaning for me by 'standing for' an idea in my mind. When I use it I simply hope it has the same meaning for you, but there is no real way of knowing. This is inadequate, so the modern rejection of empiricism offers a different way of thinking. 'Instead of saying "a word has meaning because it stands for an idea," we say "to have an idea is to *know* the meaning of a word" and knowing the meaning of a word is knowing how to use it when we communicate with each other.' Interesting though all this may be, in the long run I can't see that McCabe's precise analysis of words has very much to do with Sunday morning church attenders at a Roman Catholic Mass. Most of these congregations are just as likely to misinterpret the mode of Real Presence he meticulously analyses as to interpret it in a Catholic sense. I think most of us are empiricists. I am not saying we don't need the academics, but if the truths or mysteries they write about require such complicated, abstruse and obscure language of definition why, on earth, are we surprised and shocked when ordinary people end up believing strange things?

We should avoid calling people heretics for misinterpreting

theological language. (I once heard Metropolitan Anthony Bloom talk about heretics. He gave me a refreshing new insight into the use of the word. He described 'heresy' as a deviation from true faith in belief or practice. 'In this case,' he said, 'why do we concentrate on the intellect and not on the heart? The heretics in history are all people who were accused of misrepresenting a church doctrine by their writing or teaching; no one questioned how they lived the gospel. No one ever accuses people of heresy when they lack love and compassion. Yet the love of God and of neighbour is the great commandment.' I remember him looking hard at us and saying slowly, 'If you don't love one another you are heretics.')

I don't even attempt to pass on McCabe, or Rahner, or Pittenger's analysis of the Real Presence to my pupils. Rather I tell them that Jesus was Jewish. He wasn't acquainted with all this heady wordiness of Greek theology. He used actions and symbols, story and poetry to touch our hearts and open us to the mystery of God and his presence in our lives. The sacraments are signposts to God. I direct them to what I believe is more helpful, an awareness of the presence of God in the whole of our lives. The Eucharist is only one way we come close to God by being close to Jesus. We also come into his presence when we read Scripture; he is present when we go about our ordinary daily lives; but above all he is present when we live as Jesus lived, in love, in forgiveness of one another and in selfless service of others.

For the last two years I have focused my teaching about eucharistic celebration on the Passover grace.

> Let all God's children sit at his table,
> and drink the wine of liberation,
> and eat the bread of freedom,
> freedom from bondage and freedom from oppression,
> freedom from hunger and freedom from want,
> freedom from hatred and freedom from fear,
> freedom to think and freedom to speak,
> freedom to learn and freedom to love,

freedom to hope and freedom to rejoice,
soon, in our days, Amen.[4]

This year on the Feast of Corpus Christi we made a large poster of a host and chalice. Both were filled with the faces of children and adults, black and white, rich and poor, free and in bondage. The words on the collage read: 'You are my body. I am your life.'

Resolutions for the class-room

I have spent several days reading about Eucharist, especially about Real Presence in the sacrament. I have analysed Hans Küng, the process theology of Pittenger, Empiricism and Post-Empiricism in McCabe; I have read studies by Nicholas Lash, documents from ARCIC and returned to the Scriptures. I have come to some conclusions about my practice in the class-room. The 'textbook' I will stick with for my own guidance is a 'popular' treatment of the sacraments, *Focus on the Sacraments* by Peter Wilkinson, a priest-theologian from Liverpool.[5]

First idea

I will take a look, with the children, at the theme of Luke and banquets. I like Luke, the Gospel-writer described by Canon John Drury as the 'first great humanist'. Peter Wilkinson outlines for me the thinking behind a series of lessons:

> The Last Supper was anticipated by a number of meals that Jesus had shared with sinners and tax-collectors. When asked why he did this, Jesus replied: 'It is not the healthy who need the doctor but the sick . . . I did not come to call the virtuous but sinners.' Such meals symbolised the compassion, the risking, the reaching-out, the total caring that so marked the life of Jesus. He lived for the lost, for sinners, now he would die for them. (Page 31)

I can envisage a fine display of murals along our RE corridor. I haven't chosen festive meals as the theme because I see the

Mass as a party – that rather misleading image some preachers offer to children at first communion Masses. Party it certainly is not for them. I've chosen it because it is the biblical image.

The Jews had spoken of the golden age when God would break into history. They called it the Day of the Lord and they spoke of it in terms of a banquet: 'Here on Mount Zion the Lord Almighty will prepare a banquet for all the nations of the world – a banquet of the richest food and the finest wine' (Isaiah 25:6, GNB).

For teenagers meals can be the worst experience of community, of course. All too often it is the one meeting-point of the day when parents can broach the subjects of late nights, vegetarian diets or television habits. Either that or the teenagers simply avoid sitting down with everyone else. It *can* be the opposite: the focus of family life, the anticipated relaxation of the day. Fr Hugh Lavery (whose writing I usually admire for its poetry and sharpness of image) goes somewhat over the top when he writes:

> The most evocative symbol of shared love is the meal; an indispensable symbol. The meal is wonderfully creative, creative of community. The meal is a gesture of acceptance and an agent of transformation. Here the lonely find company, the silent become articulate and the despondent recover joy. At the meal the dead come to life; discord and dissension die.[6]

I can only imagine that Fr Lavery has never been placed next to a total bore at a wedding party – as I was last year. I began in good spirits but finished silent and despondent after listening to a self-indulgent guest who spoke for an hour about the failure of the education system because of bad teaching in comprehensive schools. He only slightly changed his monologue after he had paused to ask me what I 'did'. 'I teach in a comprehensive school' I said.

I point out the problems with banquets and parties because it shows the continual frustration a teacher has in searching for the most useful model. What seems a good idea may not be so, because of the pupils' own experiences. However, I will look at banquets through the eyes of Luke, whom Dante called 'the faithful recorder of Christ's loving kindness'. Although a writer of definite middle-class background, at home therefore with people who often entertain, Luke develops the psalmist's idea that it is the poor who are guests at the feast. Our murals can follow this theme:

- Luke 5:30; 7:39; 15:3 where Jesus eats with sinners.
- Luke 13:29 where Gentiles are invited to the feast.
- Luke 14 a whole chapter set around a meal where Jesus tells parables about banquets.
- Luke 19:1–10 where Jesus eats with Zacchaeus.
- Luke 15:11–32 the feast on the Lost Son's return.
- Luke 16:20–22 Lazarus the poor man feasts with Abraham.
- Luke 24:13–15 the resurrection meal at Emmaus.

Second idea

The resurrection story of Emmaus is the starting-point for a reflection on the most serious issue of all that emerges from the eucharistic doctrine – liberation from hunger and poverty. I should be writing this paragraph in large letters, for what on earth are all the preceding words I have written about Eucharist worth if they simply produce a cosy togetherness and neglect this deepest meaning of Christ's presence in the sacrament? How can we Christians go on and on discussing sacramental principle, mode of presence, appropriate liturgy or ordination of women when a *world is starving*? I feel so strongly about this issue that my lessons usually finish with an appeal to pupils to be practical in their Christianity. Next Easter with at least one class I will be organizing a school campaign to raise money for CAFOD or Christian Aid.

Why link this with the Emmaus story? This year I read the story with 12-year-olds. I asked them to write down whatever they wanted to say about the story. Many of the class wrote something like this: The two men were troubled and anxious about Jesus' death. They felt miserable at the failure of it all.

They walked along with this stranger who nearly said goodbye and walked away. But they were a generous pair and invited the stranger to stay for a meal. When he broke bread it reminded them of what Jesus had done and said: 'Do this in memory of me.' He had asked them to share bread with others. They learnt that whenever people share with others Jesus is made present. They jumped up with joy because they suddenly understood that Jesus was alive when people were sharing bread like he had done. 'They knew him in the breaking of bread.'

Who would a teacher be? I would, when a class show out of the blue that they have got the message you really hoped to pass on to them! They certainly understood the Emmaus story far better that the Franciscan sacristan at Emmaus did. Our pilgrim group visited Emmaus on Easter Monday and celebrated Mass there together with an Italian group that arrived at the same time. After Mass we were all invited to the sacristy to share the bread rolls blessed that day by the bishop. I took my roll and began breaking it in order to offer it to our Italian friends. The sacristan ran up to me, shouting, 'No, no, one each'!

> Come to us, Lord Jesus Christ,
> come as we search the Scriptures and see
> God's hidden purpose,
> come as we walk the lonely road, needing a companion,
> come when life mystifies and perplexes us,
> come into our disappointments and unease,
> come at table where we share our food and hopes,
> and, coming, open our eyes to recognise you.[7]

I have no doubt that I will start this practical RE project with the wonderful story related by Pauline Webb, the Methodist broadcaster. She once visited a self-help project set up by the churches in the shanty town outside Santiago, Chile. A smiling baker handed her one of his newly baked loaves saying the only English words he knew, 'Take and eat'. He remembered the words spoken by the Irish missionary who had recently celebrated

Mass for the community. She saw the invitation as a shared Eucharist. So do I.

Third idea

This is for my older students as the pressure of exam time sets in. Towards the end of one lesson we will go to the oratory. I will light a candle and in the quiet I will read them an article written by Ronald Rolheiser for the *Catholic Herald*. In it he tells the story of a young Jewish child, Mordecai, who constantly refused to attend school. His parents persuaded and threatened, even sought the help of a psychiatrist. Nothing worked. In despair they took him to an old rabbi. He listened to the parents, then without a word he picked the little boy up and held him close to his heart for a few minutes. From then on, Mordecai stayed in school. Rolheiser likens the story to the Gospel story of the woman who touched the hem of Jesus' garment. And he goes on to describe the Eucharist in the light of the two stories:

> What happens there is something beyond words and understanding, though not beyond love . . . Power is transmitted through love that goes beyond rational understanding. That is why when after Jesus had spent all his words he left us the Eucharist. That is also why after we have spent all our words we should celebrate the Eucharist. When our own words, decisions, and actions are inadequate to relive the aching in our hearts, we need the embrace of the mother, God. This happens in the Eucharist . . . Ultimately we go to the Eucharist to let ourselves be held.

The following lesson we will have a classroom Mass, priest carefully chosen, quiet, the Gospel reading – the woman who touched the hem of Jesus' garment. No sermon, no words to interrupt our meditation, we will simply enter the ritual, for as Rolheiser says, 'In it, God holds us to her heart.'

3

TRESPASSERS WILL BE FORGIVEN

Jesus comes to his friends
when they confess the wrong things they have done,
so as to marvel again at God's forgiveness.

When we first came to Norwich I found a teaching post at a Special School. It was hard work trying to understand the strange behaviour patterns of these young people who were on the fringe of life; children like John who was excluded from a series of High Schools for his disruptive behaviour, or like Sharon who had to be coaxed daily into coming to school in the constant effort to overcome her school phobia. There was Dean who sat curled up under the desk on most days, and a small 9-year-old, Laura, who would hurtle into my room and almost certainly damage some article of furniture or equipment at each visit.

One incident at this school stands out clearly in my mind as a parable of the sacrament of reconciliation. Two young girls, boarders at the school, went missing over one night. They disappeared after supper and staff, parents and police spent fourteen hours searching for them. At 9.30 a.m. as we were beginning classes the next morning, two bedraggled, frightened 10-year-olds came up the path through the trees. Their teacher saw them first and ran out, gathered them into her arms and wept with relief. Matron ushered them to the kitchen for breakfast and then settled them in bed. No angry words. No recriminations. During the afternoon the two girls, somewhat refreshed, returned to their form-room and as they arrived the other pupils spontaneously welcomed them back. They no doubt picked up their attitude from the teacher. Suddenly Michelle burst into tears, 'Why doesn't someone tell us off for what we did?' she sobbed.

We have the utmost difficulty in accepting total forgiveness because our instinctive expectation for doing wrong is to be punished. We expect to give people what they deserve and to receive, in turn, what we deserve. No wonder then, that the Christian doctrine of sin and God's forgiveness is a most challenging concept to explore. In all my years of teaching, of living both in a convent and in a parish, of attending lectures, reading or listening to sermons, I have found very few Christians who would share my view that God's forgiveness of my sins is totally independent of my repentance. He forgives because he is good and loving. He accepts me not because I am good, but because he is. This has always seemed utterly straightforward to me yet it is obviously the very opposite of the 'official' line I was taught. I still remember the catechism words we had to learn:

> *What is venial sin?*
> Venial sin is an offence which does not kill the soul, yet displeases God, and often leads to mortal sin.
> *Why is it called venial sin?*
> It is called venial sin because it is more easily pardoned than mortal sin.[1]

At 6 years old I was given a terrible impression of God: a tough, unbending figure who was always on the look out to catch me in venial sin. Then he would be very displeased and punishment would fit the crime. The ultimate horror was to be led from venial sin into mortal sin (missing Sunday Mass, for example) because that meant hell for all eternity. My mother used to tell us of her Monday morning ritual. A strict nun, Sr Ethelburga, used to line up her class of 9-year-olds, and go down the line asking which Mass they had attended on the previous day. If she suspected lying, she would question them further about the priest or the sermon. My mother lived in fear because her parents didn't go to church and she couldn't always get there on her own, although she tried. Those who failed the test were made to stand in front of the class in disgrace, with the accusation repeated week by week, 'These children are living in mortal sin.'

How Sr Ethelburga was allowed to terrify her charges in this way is beyond me. What such teaching had to do with the gospel, I don't know. I realize there are gospel texts which wave a stick at you. But they are totally outweighed by texts which speak of God as a compassionate father. Especially Luke, who had interpreted the life and death of Jesus in a way that highlighted the compassion of God. In his Gospel Luke has two favourite themes: God's attitude to the poor and his attitude to the sinner. The Gospel-writer says that God is revealed to the world in the life and death of Jesus. Look at him and you will see what God is like. I remember my mother's surprise when she read about sin and forgiveness in my first school textbook, which was based on Luke. Whether my explanation finally overcame the damage done by Sr Ethelburga I don't really know!

I have often asked my students to consider various responses that God could make to sin.

- *The thunderbolt.* God could be angry, outraged that his plans were upset and his rule disobeyed. He could respond to such anger by taking revenge and striking the sinner down.
- *The scales.* Alternatively God could be a little more controlled. Though still enraged at the disruption of his plan, he could demand justice in a cool way. He could weigh up the harm done, and then demand that strict satisfaction must be made to compensate.
- *The handshake.* God could be even less severe, in fact generous enough not to ask for strict justice. He could forgive the sinner without demanding any compensation. Instead, he would settle for the sinner's repentance and the promise that the offence will not be committed again. A contract, with a promise made by both parties.
- *The blind eye.* Finally God could be totally undemanding, prodigal in his forgiveness. This forgiveness could be so total and freely given that no conditions whatsoever are

attached. In fact, God could act towards the sinner as if no sin had been committed. In this case God's attitude wouldn't even change if the sinner repeats his wrongdoing.

When I give the class this exercise I always remind them that forgiveness of sin is one of the key Christian doctrines. I ask them to decide which of the four responses they think God makes. To help them decide I send them to a number of Luke texts (see page 68).

I am always surprised to find that the students are reluctant to choose the blind eye option, in spite of the fact that Luke points them that way. Luke makes it clear that Jesus was preaching about a God who grants people a totally free pardon from sin. In fact, he says that Jesus' own life manifested the total forgiveness of this loving God. People are forgiven not because they have repented, or because they have earned it, or because they believe, or because they are good. They are forgiven, whatever offence they have committed, simply because God is good. He always acts as though he hasn't noticed how we really are. Luke tells us to rejoice at this. And this is what the sacrament of reconciliation does.

The absoluteness of the blind eye option is perhaps too frightening to contemplate and at the same time too good to be true. It certainly frightened Michelle, the runaway schoolgirl, who couldn't cope with compassion when her whole young life had been starved of understanding and generosity from parents who had abused her. It certainly wasn't Sr Ethelburga's choice; she had obviously put her money on the second option, the God of the strict scales of justice.

Traditional Christianity has not been as severe as her. Most Christians have settled for the third option, the God of the handshake, and the practice of the Church seems to confirm them in that choice. For the Church has emphasized the three conditions necessary for forgiveness of sin in the sacrament: contrition, confession and satisfaction. The sacrament is presented as the handshake, the contract, in which both parties agree to keep their promise. It is the making up between the two parties,

God who was offended and the sinner who had offended. 'Shake and make up' is what we say, after all, to the fighting children in the playground.

In the class-room, I try to take the children further. We explore the blind eye option. First we talk about Dot Cotton in *Eastenders*. Here is a mother who finds every excuse she can for the wicked behaviour of her wayward son. She stands by him over and over again, even after he had tried to kill her. Viewers think of her as a silly woman: 'Doesn't she know what Nick is like?' Of course she does. But as Dot would say, 'He's my Nick, he's my son.' Is it possible that God could be just as doting on us?

Then we turn to Luke's Gospel. I remind the pupils of the story of the Prodigal Son. The great majority of the class will know the story well, so I don't read it from the Gospel. I retell it. But when I come to the part where the son returns home I add my own adjustments. I say something like this: 'Then the father says to his younger son, "We are delighted you are back but you must promise not to run off again. And when you have apologized for the distress you caused us all – and remember you have been most unfair to your older brother leaving him to do your share of the work – then we will put on a party . . ." '

I hardly get so far in my story because the class shout me down. 'That's not the Gospel story.' 'The father never said that.' I explain that nevertheless he must have meant that or else it wouldn't be fair; it is certainly how we act, isn't it? They quickly get the point and agree that, according to Luke, God does not act like us. He turns the blind eye. He is the prodigal one, the extraordinary parent who wastes his love and acts recklessly to welcome home the ungrateful child.

Here is another attempt to make the point:

> Jack Robinson dies, and comes face to face with God.
> 'Oh my God, I've arrived! I never thought I'd make it.'
> 'Really? Why?'
> 'You know. All those sins of mine.'
> 'Oh well, forget that now. You're most welcome.'

'But I can't forget it! Years and years of disobeying your commandments.'

'What do you mean, commandments?'

'You remember, that affair in the 1940s.'

'Oh yes. Good heavens! I'd totally forgotten about that.'

'And in 1948, those awful things I did to Jane.'

'But you confessed that, and I said, Forget it. I'd forgotten till now.'

'Not to mention a lifetime of petty lies, and dishonesty, and selfishness, and spitefulness, and of course that dreadful business in 1965.'

'Good gracious me! I'd never have remembered. But why don't you forget it all, as I've done?'

'I can't! These wounds won't heal without facing up to them. Good God! Don't you know any psychology?'

The economy of words pinpoints the problem. Even God's determination to forgive seems unable to dent the Christian's determination to be obsessed with guilt. It used to be thought that because of their practice of confession few Roman Catholics needed to see a psychiatrist. The very opposite may be true. Sr Ethelburga has seen to that! When the MP Ann Widdicombe became a Catholic recently, the *Radio Newsquiz* asked, 'Which MP is taking a crash course in guilt?' Everyone laughed. But there was no hesitation in getting the right answer.

Why can't we accept God's 'blind-eye' forgiveness? I said above that it might be too frightening to contemplate. After all, the gospel expects us to do likewise! The gospel call is to become just like Christ, in the same way as he is just like God. Matthew expresses it in the words, 'Be ye perfect as God is perfect.' The charge is so demanding that we are inclined to water it down. Even Luke felt obliged to change the wording: 'Be ye compassionate as your heavenly Father is compassionate.' But is even that watered-down perfection within our capacity?

Towards our own, perhaps, we manage it easily enough. I remember kissing our Pedro goodnight when he was about five, and whispering, 'I love you Pedro, such a lot.' He whispered back, 'But you don't love me when I'm naughty, do you?' I hugged him tight and told him that I loved him all the time, even when he was naughty. 'I don't always like the naughty things you sometimes do, but you, Ped, I love the whole time', I said. He stroked my cheek and said, 'Oh, that's nice'.

But can we extend this God-like forgiveness beyond our own family? When it costs little, perhaps. During a night-time chatter with Blanca about the same time as the Pedro episode Blanca suddenly said 'Sorry Sophie'. 'Who is Sophie?' I asked. 'I poked her at playgroup.' I was delighted to realize that Blanca was learning to consider others outside the family.

But supposing the forgiveness of others costs a lot? How forgiving would I be towards someone who had done me enormous harm or damage? I don't know. What I do know is that the gospel requires me to forgive even that. And so I am always worried by the attitude of families after court decisions concerning the tragic loss of life. In murder cases, for example, more often than not, all one hears from the bitter and angry families of the victims is 'He should be hung . . . He should rot in hell . . . Her sentence was not long enough.' Obviously I cannot appreciate how much agony they must feel. I have not been put in their terrible position, so I don't know what it is like. But I suspect that it points to lifelong misery for themselves. Such bitterness can only harm themselves and condemn their families to an imprisonment even worse than the custodial imprisonment of the murderer. Even as I write this, tonight's television news showed the family of a murder victim dancing and cheering as they left the court, exultant that the murderer got a life sentence. But what of the murderer's family? They slipped, heartbroken, into the background, themselves now the victims of a lost life.

I have two pieces of TV documentary which I show my older classes when we talk of this sacrament. The first is an interview with a lady who insists she is a Christian by conviction. Dorothy was mugged and the incident has left her fearful and unable to go out on her own. Her whole attitude to her muggers is one of revenge: 'I want done to them what they did to me. "An eye for an eye, a tooth for a tooth." ' When asked if she would ever be able to forgive them, she replied, 'No, never, absolutely never. I'm as good a Christian as anyone else. Why should I forgive them?'

Alongside this I show an interview with Gordon Wilson, the father of Marie, killed by the IRA bomb at Enniskillen. His forgiveness is genuine and total. His face is full of pain, yet soft and expressive. All I need to do is ask the class which of the two seems most damaged by their personal suffering. They recognize that Dorothy is causing damage to herself by her inability to forgive.

I remember years ago talking to Monsignor Michael Buckley on his return from a visit to Belfast where he worked on supply in a parish. He told me of an event which would never catch the headlines and yet offers a sense of hope and resurrection in the midst of the Northern Ireland tragedy. A young IRA sympathizer, Kieran, was convicted of murder. His distraught mother was in the parish where Fr Michael was acting as parish priest. One evening he answered the door to a lady who looked drawn and tired. She asked if he would take her to see Kieran's mother, as she wanted to share her sorrow. Fr Michael agreed. 'Imagine', he said to me, 'how I felt when I left them together – one, the Catholic mother of a young murderer, the other, the Protestant mother of the young victim. They were both holding hands and weeping with and for each other.'

The incident reminded me of Norma Farber's poem.

> In Mary's house the mourners gather:
> Sorrow pierces them like a nail.
> Where's Mary herself meanwhile?
> Gone to comfort Judas's mother.[2]

It is worthwhile and encouraging telling these stories to older pupils. They are sensitive and thoughtful enough to recognize the gospel Jesus in the story. It makes sense to them, even though they agree that such an ideal is very difficult to follow. For some of them it may be apparently impossible to forgive the hurt and damage already done to them by their sad family history. I was taken aback recently by the text of a paper given by Tracy Hansen to a group of Roman Catholic clergy on the subject of child sexual abuse. She had been abused at the age of six. For many years she submerged her feelings and thought she had forgiven all the hurt of the past. But when her real memory of the rape returned, thirty years after the event, she found that her simple understanding of gospel forgiveness was totally inadequate. 'To me, "forgiveness" meant that in some way I would have to excuse or condone the rape, or imply it did not matter. That would mean that I did not matter.' She found that when she tried to forgive she could only achieve 'forgiveness' by repressing all the feelings about the rape once again. In other words, forgiveness actually stood in the way of the healing process. She also had the terrible feeling that if she forgave the abuser she would expose herself again to the possibility of further abuse. Perhaps this explains Dorothy's inability to forgive her muggers. By doing so she would lay herself open to more hurt and fear.

Tracy Hansen found a way out of her corner. She discovered a new concept of forgiveness which enabled her to come to terms with her experience and start to relinquish her own sense of guilt. She found the story of Onesimus and Philemon in St Paul's letters and there understood 'forgiveness' in terms of 'cancellation of a debt'. For her the recognition that a 'debt' existed proved to her that her abuser had actually 'stolen' from her. It made her accept that she was the victim, not an accomplice; that she was 'trespassed against' and therefore that she had a right to repayment. Much later Tracy realized that she could be set free from the burden of thirty years if she took the initiative and voluntarily cancelled the debt that the rapist owed her. It left her in charge, and her self-image restored.

I hope Tracy's story and solution will help my teenagers who find themselves in a similar situation. Even so, I can't pretend that I find it easy to talk with young people about forgiveness. And if I find it uncomfortable, how much more difficult it has always been for primary school teachers. In our Catholic schools they are asked to prepare children to receive this sacrament of reconciliation at the age of seven. The age is significant. It corresponds, apparently, to the 'age of reason'. By her seventh birthday a child should be capable of knowing what sin is, who God is, and be capable to seriously offending him. Like the new school test for 7-year-olds, it takes no account of the wide span of emotional, social and intellectual maturation between children of this age. Nor does it distinguish between boys and girls, when it is a fact that girls mature much quicker than boys.

It was really only as a parent that I became aware of all this. I began to ask many questions about the wisdom of our Church in selecting the age of seven for 'first confessions'. In my diocese it is still the practice to prepare children for this sacrament before their first communion. It soon became evident to me that if our children were growing up learning about God's forgiveness from us, then any sacramental expression of it should be a celebration of God's love, not an examination of conscience and a nervous interview with a comparative stranger in the church. I made the mistake of expressing this opinion at a parents' meeting. The priest in charge was shocked at my views and said, 'Children aged seven can commit SIN [he emphasized the word], serious SIN.' Since I had done a bit of reading on the matter, I stuck to my guns. Was it not true that the practice of weekly 'confession' he was advocating was a late introduction (twelfth century) to church tradition? And did not the recent Vatican Council recommend a rethink and revision of sacramental practice? I wasn't dismissing a celebration. I just wanted it to be a different experience from the one I had myself had as a child. He simply dismissed me as a trouble-maker, and in such dogmatic terms that none of the other parents dared to support me. I left the meeting near to tears, utterly frustrated that our experience as parents counted for nothing to this priest. Yet I was expected to entrust my children to him in the delicate area of their behaviour and their relationship to God.

Thank God that priest represented only one view. There are priests who have adopted more sympathetic practices in the celebration of the sacrament, and they give me heart. Peter Wilkinson has written the best analysis of the rite of reconciliation that I have seen. In *Focus on the Sacraments* (published in

1987, the same year as my children received the sacrament) he expressed clearly and sensitively everything I had raised at my parish meeting:

> The sacrament of confession, in the experience of many people, had belonged to a spirituality which reflected an obsession with sin and a sense of being overwhelmed by feelings of guilt. It encouraged within people a very poor image of themselves, with little experience of forgiveness and the sense of being accepted. People were well able to identify with St Peter's words: 'Depart from me, O Lord, for I am a sinful man'. They tended to regard God as a stern and stony God of endless demand and infinite reprisal, a God who condemns for repeated failure.
>
> In the experience of Gerard Hughes, such a spirituality has caused mental breakdown and disillusionment, has fuelled anxiety neuroses, stunted moral development and has so filled some people with guilt that they now feel bad about being good, and all spontaneity, delight and joy has been banished from their lives (cf. *God of Surprises*, p. 67). What a different God emerges from the pages of the Scriptures![3]

I can vouch for the accuracy of this analysis. My children, like most of their peer group, have not the slightest inclination to continue the practice of 'confession'. In my plea for a celebration of God's loving acceptance and forgiveness of us as we are, I had included in my article for a well-known Catholic journal (already mentioned on page 35) a comment about the timing of first confession:

> Very soon Pedro and Blanca will start to prepare for their first confession. I already fear that this Catholic practice may not be all that helpful to them. Why start talking 'sin' language to children who can never offend God? They only know how to disturb the peace and try the patience of adults around them. Is that sin? The other evening Blanca and her daddy argued before bedtime. She was only being high-spirited, and her boisterous behaviour disturbed a very

> tired and busy father. He was really cross and she went to bed in tears. Bert regretted his impatience all evening and early in the morning told Blanca that he was sorry for his cross words. 'Oh, that's alright Daddy,' she said, hugging him, 'I love you.' Now if that isn't a family celebration of God's forgiving love, I don't know what is. This is where we find God, and we don't even need to mention his name.

This also surprised and worried the editor, who replied in his refusal to publish: 'You ask why we should talk "sin" language to children. But why not? Are you right to say that children could never offend God? What about the cruelty to each other and to their parents of which they are capable?'

This is a complex area of morality, I admit. In the light of the 1993 murder of a Liverpool 3-year-old by two 10-year-olds, it would be foolish to suggest that all children are totally innocent, though I question in those cases where the guilt lies. I will return to that question later. But I still stand by my argument that the ordinary 7-year-old child, brought by practising Catholic parents to the sacraments, is not capable of the serious rejection of God that the term 'sin' implies. They can be selfish, yes. They can be greedy, yes. They can argue with parents and siblings, yes. They may tell lies sometimes, yes. And they need to grow out of this behaviour. But parents should know that the psychologists identify this behaviour as the normal responses of a developing child to their expanding world. They are testing it. Moreover, the behaviour of children is likely to be a copy of that of the parents or other influential adults. Children, for example, who yell and shout to get their own way have learnt that behaviour from adults. So who is at fault?

Teachers are in a good position to observe the development of children, and therefore to offer an opinion to priests about the advisability of first confession and its frequent practice. One headteacher wrote to the Catholic press that after twenty-three years of rather 'unsympathetically' witnessing his teachers preparing 7-year-olds for this sacrament, he found himself having to take classes himself. He wrote:

> Before the second lesson was over, I realized what agonies Catholic infant teachers, especially if they had children of their own, must suffer. I have given one lesson so far in which I struggled to separate out the ideas of 'rule breaking', 'offending against social behaviour' and sin as a 'deliberate, wilful, conscious act of disobedience against God', and frankly cannot and will not believe that ANY child is either capable of such a thing or indeed would ever wish it. Therefore – what precisely is this seven-year-old going to confess when he comes to make his 'first confession'? Probably at the risk of losing my job, I am going to refuse this year to teach something I do not hold with any longer.[4]

I repeat the point I made earlier. Neither the headmaster nor I mix with children likely to hit the headlines for mugging the elderly, or for stealing cars and killing innocent pedestrians, or for terrorizing the neighbourhood. Perhaps if we lived in deprived inner-city areas where unemployment is way above national average we would write differently. Yet even so, we wouldn't describe such children as criminals. Even our legal system agrees on that. Their behaviour is unacceptable. But that does not mean it is their fault.

Nor is it children like these who are the most likely to be presented for the sacraments. The legislation is for children of practising Catholics and I know none who would call their children sinners. Children certainly know, as I have said, how to disturb the peace and try the patience of adults around them. But sin is too fierce a word to apply. Even Herbert McCabe's *New Catechism* makes no mention of childish behaviour in the chapter on Penance. The sacrament, for him, is a 'welcoming back from grave sin'. That is an adult matter.

I am glad to say that the Church has, in fact addressed this whole issue in recent years. For centuries the emphasis on the sacrament was confession, with the priest assuming the role of judge. It led to so much fear and scrupulosity that the healing love of God was obscured. The sacrament was reformed at the Second Vatican Council and renamed as the sacrament of *reconcili-*

ation. The very private celebration of confession had obscured the social nature of sin, where relationships with one another are damaged. The new name is intended to highlight this aspect of sin.

Since Vatican II, Catholics are less likely to put sins in two simplistic categories, venial and mortal. I remember years ago being present at an Orthodox parish discussion group in Metropolitan Anthony Bloom's house. I was asked to give the Roman Catholic view on the difference between venial and mortal sins. 'Venial sins are the ordinary, everyday wrongdoings,' I said, 'the lies, the cheating, the unkindnesses that we all fail in. Mortal sin is much more serious. It is "deadly" because it is a deliberate turning away from God. It cuts the person right off from God.' I asked Anthony Bloom how he would describe venial and mortal sin. He paused for a moment and then said: 'Two penitents went to a holy monk in the desert. One confessed to a single, terrible sin. The monk sent her out into the desert to search for the heaviest stone she could manage to bring back to his hut. The other confessed to numerous small failings. They counted them all: 256. The monk told her to go into the desert and collect 256 small stones. When she returned with them, the monk told both penitents to go back and replace the stones exactly where they had been found.' Clearly for him, sinfulness consists as much in restorability as in size.

The Vatican Council also allowed for some experimentation with new ways of celebrating the forgiveness of God. A *New Rite of Penance and Reconciliation* was devised which encouraged a more relaxed human relationship between priest and penitent. Many parishes changed the confession box into a small, comfortable room where the priest and penitent could meet face to face. The 'confession' takes the form of a prayerful conversation between the two. Some Catholics have abandoned the practice of private confession altogether. They prefer a form of the new rite which provides for a group celebration of penitence to emphasize the communal nature of sin and forgiveness. There are two forms of this rite, one where those present conclude the community celebration with a brief private confession and the second which concludes with a general absolution. The latter is restricted to areas where there are few priests, but many Catholics would like to see it made more widely available.

In 1983 Pope John Paul II convened a sixth Synod of Bishops to consider 'Reconciliation and Penance in the Mission of the Church'. It was to be an exchange of ideas, 'a learning situation' the Pope called it, about the Church's attitude towards reconciliation with God and the world. The media quickly interpreted it as a move to restore private confession, which was allegedly threatened with extinction in some parts of the world by the practice of general absolution. Some bishops went to Rome determined that the Synod should focus on the social aspects of reconciliation. Third-World bishops, prominent in calling for justice and peace in the world, were calling for a reconciliation which divided the world's resources equitably. One commentator announced, 'Mark my words, within days the Synod will be dealing with only two things: general absolution and the social ethics of multi-nationals.'

In the event, the five days of speeches from one country after another did produce a balance between reflections on individual sin and on what was called 'social sin'. The working paper for the Synod had seemed to suggest that reconciliation with God (from individual sin) must come first if there was to be some chance of solving the sinful situations of the world. I was delighted to discover that our own Archbishop Worlock of Liverpool spoke early in the debate to argue the opposite. He describes his argument in these words:

> I reminded the Fathers of Pope Paul VI's words, that mankind is called to find his God through loving and serving his fellow human beings. In this way the Pope had said, 'Our humanism becomes Christianity and our Christianity becomes centred on God: in such sort that we may say that a knowledge of man is a pre-requisite for a knowledge of God.' This, I argued, was true also of reconciliation. We must start with the complex longings of the human heart. The search for social justice could lead to a desire for

> reconciliation with God. It is the changing needs of people, real and psychological, which have led to the development over the centuries of the way in which the sacrament has been celebrated.[5]

I am heartened by the fact that bishop after bishop called for the same concentration on social justice. Cardinal Gantin of West Africa called for solidarity with the poor. Cardinal Lorscheider of Brazil called the identification with the poor one of the true marks of the Church in its ministry of reconciliation. Indian bishops expressed concern about the acceptance of the caste system and the poverty in which it kept people. Archbishop Henry D'Souza spoke with passion of the structural sin which he identified as the inheritance of colonialism. The sin of injustice and violence against the people was echoed over and over again from Latin American bishops. North American and European bishops concentrated on the need for reconciliation with other Christians and other faiths. Cardinal Willebrands quoted the Pope himself who had said, 'The sin of disunity amongst Christians weighs heavily on the Church.'

A French cardinal spoke with feeling for the Jewish people: 'We have a mission of repentance for our secular attitudes towards the Jewish people . . . We must know how to seek forgiveness of Our Lord and our brothers who have been plunged into the horror of the holocaust.' Bishop Conti of Aberdeen spoke of the corporate effort needed to reconcile people and nations, and called upon governments to devote more effort and more money to solve consequences of mass unemployment. 'As I speak', he said, 'in all probability a submarine is leaving Holy Loch in Scotland armed with Polaris missiles, capable of destroying the cities of Russia and their entire populations. Each day we spend here, ten thousand people die of starvation in the Third World.'

I am grateful to Archbishop Worlock for recording these observations of some of our Catholic bishops. The hierarchy is all too often stereotyped as a rigid, uncreative group of thinkers, anxious to preserve the status quo. In fact many called for fundamental changes in our attitude towards sin. Many of them actually pleaded for the retention of the general absolution rite, and even for its extension into more common use. It was Cardinal Ratzinger who put on the brakes here, invoking the teaching of the Council of Trent 450 years ago, according to which divine law requires every grave sin to be confessed individually to a priest.

Over the past thirty years a new, more communal theology of sin has developed. Original sin is no longer seen as a stain on the soul inherited from our forefather Adam. Rather it is the sinful situation of the world into which people are born. Teachers who have adopted this way of describing sin are often criticized. 'You don't teach about sin any more', we are frequently told, not least by politicians who are happy to blame the decline in social behaviour on bad teachers and weak leadership in the churches. If only they knew just how seriously we do take the reality of sin. True, we no longer get children to learn catechism questions, or fill them with guilt by giving them lists of all the wrong doings they could do. (I remember too well how often I had to make up faults to provide a 'worthwhile' list for my Saturday confession!) But we do teach them about our communal human responsibility for one another. We do teach them that there can be no purely private sins: 'Every sin, no matter how seemingly private and not harming anyone, makes us less a bearer of Christ for one another.'

Our critics seems to have a nostalgia for the time when behaviour was inspired by fear and guilt. We would prefer behaviour to be inspired by love and responsibility, out of respect for all of God's creation. In school RE today we lead our pupils to become aware of the sinful situation of the world, and we seek to inspire them to respond in generosity to change that situation. This is far more demanding of them than anything I was given in my childhood. It can result in young Catholics like Sean Deveraux leaving behind a life of comfort for the danger and discomfort of Mogadishu (where he was murdered for his love of justice and his devotion to the poor). It can inspire Daniella, a former pupil of our school, to put her university career on hold whilst she flies out to Recife in Brazil to the street children who have won her heart. It can inspire several of our sixth-formers to give up their summer holiday with its chance to earn money, to go to India and Africa to work on voluntary projects with the De La Salle Brothers. It means, above all, that the whole school in its actual mission is orientated towards concern for others. I have to say that this is a refreshing reversal of the Thatcherite values ('Put yourself first and go for it' is how one of my students describes it) which continue to blight our country.

Our way of teaching inevitably brings criticism because it makes our young students fairly vocal in their opposition to social injustice, especially when it takes place under our own noses. I was teaching a series of classes for sixth-formers on peace and justice issues, at the time of the dispute with the Education Minister over the publication of test results. I was taken aback by the vehemence of their opposition to his proposals. So I wrote to him.

Dear Mr Patten,

I am a distressed RE teacher. You will be pleased to know that our RE GCSE exams are so successful that nearly 40 students have chosen to take an A-level examination in Christian philosophy and ethics.

My distress is this. These sixth-formers have expressed to me their deep concern that you, a Catholic Minister of Education, can put your name to the practice of publishing and comparing exam results. This public humiliation of the under-privileged, socially deprived, racially disadvantaged and less academically able pupils is contrary to our Christian values. They find this incompatible with your inaugural statement as Education Minister of the need for a return to neglected Christian values of morality.

The basis of our Christian teaching is that all our pupils are worthy of respect. To pick out high academic achievement as more worthy than other gifts is contrary to everything our schools stand for. But as one student put it – 'In the eyes of the Government the only people who are worthwhile are those who can earn a lot of money'.

I left college, years ago, with the advice of my principal firmly in my heart: 'Never ever humiliate your less academic pupils by pining up test results on the notice-board. Remember that Jesus preferred to stand alongside those who struggled. Walk with all your pupils, don't run away with the achievers.'

Can you suggest how I should respond to my sixth-formers who believe that you have really no time for those who can only walk? They believe, as I do, that this is contrary to Christian ethics.

We would really like to discuss this with you. Is there any chance of you visiting us? If not we would be grateful for a personal reply.

Yours sincerely . . .

I had seriously imagined that he might reply, and perhaps even visit us for a healthy discussion of the issue. What wishful thinking. All we got was a patronizing reply from the DES five months later, written by an under secretary whose only vision was on raising standards at all costs. The letter didn't address the issue at all, perhaps because no one at the DES understood it. Thank goodness there are some who do understand the teaching profession. Here is the comment of Brian Thorne, Director of the Centre for Counselling Studies at the University of East Anglia:

> Behind the current battle over testing in our schools and aside from the very real issues of excessive work demands on teachers, there resides, I suspect, a profoundly more significant and symbolic struggle. Raising standards, improving the quality of teaching, providing evidence of achievement – they all sound worthy objectives and they appeal to those who relish hitting targets and obtaining hard data. But many teachers know – even those who find it difficult to express themselves with adequate feeling – that learning depends ultimately on love, love between teachers and taught and love for the subjects that are being studied. Testing is about judgement and where that judgement is divorced from the relationship between pupil and teacher,

> then the spirit of learning easily withers and trust ebbs away. What is more when testing becomes the principal cornerstone of the educational edifice then the building loses warmth and becomes inhospitable and eventually uninhabitable. The battle over testing is about loss of love, loss of tenderness, loss of imagination, loss of trust, loss of soul. And the sad thing is that those words of mine will make no sense to those who believe that they are right and I am a woolly minded liberal whose gravest misfortune was to have been educated in the 1950s and brainwashed in the 1960s. What is more I have to struggle with the knowledge that the present Minister of Education is a devoted and often charming Roman Catholic, a struggle made somewhat more distasteful by the realisation, if I am to believe what is reported in the press, that he holds to doctrines of original sin and of divine reward and punishment which would not have disgraced advisers to the Holy Inquisition.

If our students are becoming more critical of government as they grow in social and political sensitivity, it is not surprising they are becoming even more critical of the Church. The reaction of my students to Archbishop Worlock's revelation of the bishops' concern for social justice is likely to be somewhat sceptical. 'Hypocrites', I can hear them say. 'Who has been more responsible for injustices across the world and across the centuries than the Church?' No doubt they will point to our messy history, where popes and other leaders have given little example and inspiration to the faithful. They will point to the terrible missionary exploitation of the Indian people of Latin America, not to mention discrimination against women that has disgraced the Church for centuries. They will undoubtedly point to the church cover-ups to protect bishops who sire children and priests who abuse altar servers. I can only offer these disheartened young people the hope that all is not lost for the Church. The Church, after all, is the people, a struggling, unfaithful community in need constantly of forgiveness, not seven times but seventy times seven times. I will let Peter Wilkinson have the last word:

The sacrament points to an essential aspect of the nature of the Church itself: it must be recognised as the source of forgiveness and reconciliation. We must forgive as we have been forgiven, called to be ambassadors for Christ in the work of reconciliation.

This must be true, first and foremost, within the Church if we are to proclaim the Gospel effectively. We need to acknowledge the hurt that has caused so much bitterness in the lives of many of our own people. They include priests who have left the active ministry, the divorced and remarried, young people and women whose gifts have not been recognised, and many others who did not receive the helping hand when they needed it most. If we are truly the body of Christ we must constantly touch the lives of all these people with the generosity of Christ.[6]

Resolutions for the class-room

***First idea** (for 15-year-olds)*

Study all the Luke texts as an introduction to a reflection on 'The sort of God I believe in'. First of all the pupils will study the chart below and then we will meet in the oratory to have a prayerful reflection on the theme.

	God's attitude towards the sinner
Luke 5:29–32	Jesus was most at home with outcasts.
Luke 6:27–38	Jesus suggests that our attitude to sinners should be one of total forgiveness.
Luke 6:36	Compare this verse with Matthew 5:48.
Luke 7:36–50	Simon rejects a sinner, but Jesus sees beyond the sin and accepts the person.
Luke 9:51–6	Jesus rebuked James and John for being unforgiving.
Luke 11:2–4	Jesus presumes that we forgive others. Verse 4 is a reference to Deuteronomy 15:1.
Luke 15	Three parables that tell of God's joy in accepting sinners.

Luke 19:1–10	Zacchaeus reformed because of Jesus' welcome.
Luke 23:32–49	Jesus forgave his persecutors. Christians say, 'That is how God is'.

This will lead to a discussion on the four types of God: the thunderbolt, the scales, the handshake, the blind eye.

***Second idea** (for 12-year-olds)*

We will prepare a reconciliation service for Lent. Our school chaplains tell us that secondary pupils today, with their strong attraction to the peer group, are happy to go to the priest in groups for communal confessions.

After choosing an overall theme I will divide my class into groups and give them tasks: (1) to prepare the oratory in an imaginative way; (2) to choose and set up the music – possibly from their modern, popular music stars; (3) to choose readings from Scripture and other sources; (4) to choose or compose prayers of repentance and reconciliation; (5) to suggest one practical resolution as a class action for Lent.

When we have celebrated our communal service with the chaplain, I will offer each group time to see him if they wish.

***Third idea** (for sixth-formers)*

I think it would be worthwhile to make a study of the 1983 Sixth Synod of Bishops, 'Reconciliation and Penance in the Mission of the Church'. The study would be based on Archbishop Worlock's pamphlet *Repent and Believe.*

Each student would have a copy and a questionnaire to answer, based on the following themes:

- The nature and practical working of a synod.
- The general debate, examples from the world-wide Church.
- Reconciliation with God (private confession).
- Reconciliation with the world (general confession).
- The results of the synod.

The second part of the study would involve a discussion with invited speakers, including (I hope) a bishop or his representative.

The third part of the study would result from the earlier sessions and would involve creating a large mural illustrating the social aspect of sin.

4

GROWING UP

Jesus comes to his friends
when they 'confirm' their baptism by
promising to live as Jesus did, in his Spirit.

When does a Christian grow up? Have I grown up in my faith? Can I call myself a mature Christian? We talk to our children as they prepare for confirmation about growing up and making their own personal commitment to Christ. We presume that by this age they are mature enough in their belief to know what they are taking on in promising to live as Jesus did. I wonder. I was just seven years old when I began this confirmed part of my Christian pilgrimage. In pre-Vatican II days the local bishop visited a parish about every four years. When he did so, all the children who had received their communion since the last visit were gathered up and confirmed. Bishop Matthews happened to visit my parish only days after my first communion. I remember absolutely nothing of the occasion, except that the bishop was short and fat.

This sacrament is intended to bring its recipient into communion with the life-giving Spirit of God. There is a certain ambiguity about this. How can it possibly add anything to our baptism? Indeed, in the early Church (as in the Eastern Churches today) it was never separated from baptism. The sacrament only emerged as a separate rite when the Western Church began to stress that it was important for the bishop to administer the rite. It was Pope Innocent I who made that rule in AD 416. But once confirmation ceased to be part of the rite of baptism, it became difficult to see why it was needed at all. Over the centuries many people were simply never confirmed until, in the thirteenth century, parents were commanded by church authority (under imposed penalties) to present children for confirmation. From that time onwards confirmation was presumed to be a vital step in the ongoing process of initiation. Without it baptism was somehow not complete. And yet it is obvious that not only confirmation, but all the sacraments, the Eucharist in particular, help to bring our baptism to completion. And presumably an even more important way of reaffirming our baptism is by responding faithfully to the call of Christ in our daily lives.

These days, confirmation is conferred later, rather than earlier. It is now considered a sacrament of Christian maturity and especially a sacrament of adolescence. It symbolizes the awakening of young people to a personal faith as they emerge into adulthood. In this chapter I want to look at two aspects of this growth in maturity. First I will look at our individual growing and 'coming of age' as disciples of Christ; and then I want to apply this thinking to the whole Church, and ask how the whole community grows in a fuller and more mature understanding of the gospel.

Last year my own children were confirmed, along with their class mates, as they prepared to move into the high school. The children were twelve years old, not yet old enough to baby-sit for friends or legally to be left alone for hours in the house, nor even allowed, by law, to take on 'after-school' work.

Yet the thinking seemed sensible: a point of growth had been reached where children were moving into the larger world of secondary education – a moment of importance and seriousness and choice. Not a bad moment for our Catholic children to give some serious thought to their faith. At the time of her confirmation Blanca was asked to write her reflections on RE by a school governor who was preparing background material for a diocesan conference on RE. My daughter has allowed me to quote her thoughts in this book.

RE is education in religion. It's about God, Jesus and his disciples and the stories about him. It's also about caring for other people – like CAFOD or street children in Brazil. Priests come into our school to say Mass and talk about God. So RE is about Church.

On the whole I prefer home RE, by this I mean talking things over with my parents and going to church in order to play music with Dad's folk group. I never listen to things the priests say because it is too boring. My favourite parts of the mass are: Sign of Peace, the Offertory procession and Communion (then I know it is near the end). In school my favourite priest for mass is Fr John Drury. He is more homely and makes us laugh. The school Masses I like most are at the end of the year and Christmas. I think this is because to me it feels good to have a Mass at the end of a hard year's work. It is a real celebration and seems more fun.

School assemblies are really a part of our RE. They have a message. I can understand this more than having churchy gospel stories. Mr Conroy's assemblies are just brilliant. When we did our Passion Play last year it was the best RE about Jesus I have ever learnt. I can still remember the story clearly. Assemblies don't always mention God or Jesus but are on subjects like forgiveness, loving and caring about the environment. This is what RE is about.

RE in class lessons doesn't interest me very much – but then we haven't done any since Christmas (Well, we did talk about prayer during Lent). Some of our RE lessons we had last year were alright, but not marvellous. We talked about our family and baptisms making us part of the community. I liked drawing the pictures because I like art. Every week we have one lesson with Mr Conroy. His RE is brilliant. He gets us involved in our world today and isn't too 'holy'. It is about caring for each other. He makes us try and think how other people feel. At the moment we are learning about prejudices. He made us write down as many examples of prejudice as we could. And we had to draw the idea in a creative way.

My mum and dad are RE teachers. I like the sound of things mum does at Notre Dame. They don't sound too churchy and holy. Mum brought a class of year 8 to visit us. They did an assembly on the Street Children of Brazil and asked us to take part in a petition to help them. They left pictures and notices for us to see. I'm very disappointed that we haven't done anything about it yet. Mum's classes also enter BBC schools competition for RE. The children have fun making newspapers about caring for people. They go out and take photographs and even went to interview Norwich City footballers. Another good idea was when some year 8 pupils made a cardboard city and sat in it every break to remind the school of the homeless in Norwich. One class made a video about the two cathedrals in Norwich. I would like this school to do things like this.

Part of my RE in school this year is to prepare for the sacrament of confirmation. I have to say I find it very boring listening to people talk on and on about the Bible because it sounds as though Jesus is a goody-goody and we are supposed to be the same. What I hear is going in one ear and out of the other. At times it sounds as though Jesus is like Paul Daniels because he can get bread out of nowhere. I find it hard to believe that Jesus could give blind people their sight or bring people back from dead. When they say he was human like us, was he?

Of course, people might think I should be chucked out of my confirmation class for writing like this. But I understand my confirmation as choosing to be a loving and caring person like Jesus was and like Mr Conroy teaches us.

(*Blanca Richards, aged 12*)

In this last sentence my daughter proves to me that she does indeed have a maturity of faith, in the vital sense that she has grasped the essence of the gospel. I am very proud of her and in deepest admiration of her very special teacher, Mr Conroy. She has yet to learn, as we all have, what it really costs to be 'a loving and caring person' all the time. The call to follow Jesus is, according to Mark, a call to martyrdom, an invitation to become 'Good Friday People', to use Sheila Cassidy's phrase. It is costly to be a follower of Christ and I am only just realizing what the currency is.

In my youth a true Catholic was measured by faithful church-going or by involvement in parish liturgy. The daily Mass-goer and the leading altar-server were accepted as the most faithful lay followers of the gospel Jesus. (Really serious Catholics would, of course, enter the priesthood or religious life.) The cost of Catholicism was attendance at Mass and blind acceptance of dogma and church law.

I've changed my currency. I don't see this blind obedience to authority as the cost of true discipleship any more. I see the currency as a faithful, never-ending struggle to put other people first – as Jesus did in his rather ordinary life as a carpenter-preacher. It sounds so simple, but it is the most difficult thing to do. It never stops and it hurts.

I was shaken many years ago by a friend, a tired mother of six teenage children. 'It must be wonderful to be a real Christian', she said. 'The priests and nuns have time for quietness and prayer, they can serve God properly. I can't because I'm too busy and exhausted for prayer.' I was shocked because she is an intelligent woman, an experienced and successful teacher and a wonderfully caring wife and mother. Her Catholic upbringing had taught her that because she was not spending every week on her knees or going to daily church, she was a second-class Christian. Ann was used to putting herself last, as most mothers are, and rarely found time or leisure to reflect and pray. She saw this as a mark against true discipleship. I would call it the very essence of her Christian witness.

The problem is that it sounds too simple to be convincing. Would I be accused of watering down Christianity if I focused all my teaching on this one, essential fact as the essence of the Gospels? Should Jesus himself be criticized for reducing his understanding of things to a single thought: 'You must love God and love your neighbour as you love yourself'? What does this actually mean to me – at this moment – on a Saturday morning in July? It is thirty minutes since I wrote the last sentence. I have been sitting still, thinking about yesterday when I left school, cross and frustrated by the end-of-term pressure and the inter-staff conflicts which always emerge when we are fighting for our own corner. I have recently been appointed Head of Department. This means a lot of pre-planning for next year, at a time when I am already inundated with reports, teacher appraisal, endless professional meetings and the ever-growing mountain of paper work resulting from government 'reforms'. (Not to mention trying to get this book finished.) New staff need to be appointed for next term, but my own and other appointments came too late for us to find the right replacements, and we are left with timetable problems, emergency solutions and the prospect of difficult times ahead. I have felt particularly let down by colleagues, who seem to be unaware of my needs, and unready to offer me, in my precarious new role, helpful advice or consideration. I have felt angry that decisions are being made about my teaching environment about which I have no say.

In the midst of this turmoil, I went along last night to a staff farewell party, and suddenly realized that all my colleagues were just as weary as I was. I noticed in particular the tired face of a senior teacher, with whom I have had more than one tussle. I suddenly saw him as a fellow human being just as worn out (no, more so, in fact) than me, and in need of my consideration and understanding. In his job he can please no one! Blanca's words about being a loving and caring person like Jesus was came back to me. Putting the needs of other people first, loving and considering them as you would like them to consider you. That's the mature thing.

This may sound as if I've decided to let everyone walk over me. Not so. I have to speak out for what I believe is in the best interests of my department, my colleagues and myself. But I have to have the maturity to see the whole picture and put myself in other people's shoes. Sr Mary, my headteacher, and one of the most mature Christian women I know, put this into words in an anecdote she recalled at a staff dinner recently. She remembered a stormy meeting she had held with the science teachers. It was in the early days of curriculum change and opinions were running very high over the options that science departments could take. There was anger and shouting and upset. As Mary left the meeting she was so disheartened that she felt near to resignation. Then Jackie, an enthusiastic member of the science team, ran after her and exclaimed; 'Sr Mary, wasn't that absolutely marvellous?' The air had been cleared.

Our Christian faith and commitment has to be lived out at this day-to-day level, amongst family and colleagues. It is human and ordinary, rough and unpolished. In all that we do, we seek the face of God alongside many other searchers.

It needs a certain amount of maturity to come to terms with this. Some people are fearful that when we express our faith in such ordinary and secular terms, we have settled for mere humanism. The topic was discussed in a recent cri-de-coeur from an Oxford undergraduate writing in *The Tablet*. She complained that the religious education she received from the Sacred Heart Sisters consisted entirely of 'caring for others, community, justice, overseas aid and political exploitation'. She recognized that the Sisters were trying to move away from the intolerable air of superiority assumed by Catholics of a past age, and to adopt a more ecumenical attitude towards those, Christian or not, who were concerned about the same human problems. But she yearned for structure, for doctrine, for dogma, for 'a specifically Catholic handle' on the things she believed in. She wrote:

> It is just not right that people should take their baptismal promises on their own heads (confirmation), and enter the Church as responsible adults, when they have no idea what it is they are professing to believe. Unless teachers are prepared to set the challenge of Christian doctrine before young people, they cannot expect them of their own accord to seek answers to questions they do not know exist. I am behind ecumenism, like most modern Christians; but how

> can we patch up our differences, if we do not know what they are?[1]

Louise was eighteen when she wrote this article and I wonder if I recognize in her writing a characteristic I trace in my own students. We RE teachers sigh with weariness when sixth-form tutors or others say, 'Have our pupils come all this way through the Catholic school system without ever having heard about Moses and the Exodus, or the Sacraments or the meaning of the Mass?' Yes, they did study all these aspects of their religion, but they only 'took in' what they wanted to or were ready to hear at the time. Louise's Sisters of the Sacred Heart may well have spoken many times on 'what the Church teaches' and yet she may be correct in saying that she never heard it! Apart from returning to catechism learning of stiff, unintelligible statements, I fail to see what more her teachers could do.

Perhaps it is proof of this young writer's immaturity that she felt threatened by the Sisters presenting themselves 'as no more than equal searchers with Buddhists and Hindus among whom they work'. (Her interpretation – I don't know how the Sisters presented themselves.) Some Christians are highly fearful of inter-faith and inter-church dialogue. Fear is always the result of insecurity. I strongly believe that mature religious people are those who are comfortable enough to mix with, to question, and to listen to people of other faiths or denominations. Mature religious people are those who can listen with absolute openness to others, without feeling threatened by their views. They recognize that we learn from one another and strengthen our own personal faith by respecting other people's beliefs. Three people I know come instantly to mind.

Rabbi Blue is every inch a committed Jewish rabbi. He never, for one moment, compromises his Jewishness by his warm and close relationship to the Christian Churches. He joyfully tells of his close friendship with many a Catholic community and recognizes the Christian influences on his own Jewish faith.

In reverse, Bert, my husband, has studied Judaism for many years. So closely has he identified with the Jewish faith and the richness of the Jewish sacred writings that one elderly nun on hearing him speak on a radio programme is reputed to have said, 'That young rabbi is very close to the Church.' Bert's love of the Jewish Scriptures, his friendship with Jewish people, his strong awareness of the Jewishness of Jesus, and his love for the Holy Land – these have only served to increase his Christian faith, not to weaken it.

One of the most interesting, and I would say 'holy', Christians I have ever known is Donald Nicholl, a man so open to others that his writings are a tapestry of riches gleaned from his dialogue with peoples of all faiths and denominations. He has a great capacity to listen with a readiness to learn from others, especially from the Eastern Orthodox Churches. Yet he remains a Catholic Christian as he has always been. He is, however, enriched and deepened by his readiness to listen for God's voice in everyone.

What a tragedy when some of our Conservative Party pro-Christian lobby, led by Baroness Cox, do all they can to suppress multi-faith education in schools. What a scandal when a Birmingham Catholic school refuses to offer a room for local Muslims to pray their Friday devotions. What a sadness that one of my RE colleagues in a local state school told us, 'One committed Christian parent has accused me of being part of the works of Satan because I teach other religions. Another recently said he could just about cope with other religions provided I made it clear that Christianity is the one ultimately true religion and that the others are false and misguided.' Jenny went on to point out the almost impossible position of the state comprehensive RE teacher: 'Atheists, agnostics and Buddhists tell me they would withdraw their children if RE became exclusively or predominantly Christian.' She cannot win whatever she does.

The great sadness of insecure people is their inability to change and accommodate. Change always implies a risk of faith. Insecure people believe that faith is somehow totally comprehensible and static. It is kept safe that way, you know what you've got. A story is told of the young Fr Heenan who, whilst a curate in East London, planted an acorn in the presbytery garden. He returned years later as the Cardinal Archbishop of Westminster and was absolutely delighted to see it had grown into a giant oak.

This brings me to the second part of this chapter. I want to widen my discussion of maturity, and ask not only how individual Christians grow into adults, but how the Church as a whole 'confirms' its baptismal commitment to Christ, and so grows day by day into a new maturity. Perhaps the first thing to note is that a pilgrim Church follows Jesus along the road to Calvary. Fr Miguel D'Escoto of Nicaragua puts this into perspective:

> I don't think we Christians have understood what carrying the cross means. We are not carrying the cross when we are poor or sick or suffering small everyday things – these are all parts of life. The cross comes when we try to change things. That is how it came for Jesus.

Change, it is being suggested, is the litmus test of fidelity to the gospel. Not change for change's sake, obviously, but the painful change that is always involved in responding to changing circumstances. An unchanging Church cannot be a mature reflection of the Christian gospel.

The changing circumstances of our own recent history have given rise to the phenomenon known as liberation theology. To what extent is this new understanding and living of the gospel an example of the Church becoming more mature?

Liberation theology has been defined in the following terms by CAFOD, the Roman Catholic organization that works to improve life for people in Third-World countries:

> The attempt to practise the Christian faith in situations of political, economic and social injustice. It poses a challenge to Christians world-wide because it demands change. It seeks the ultimate liberation of both rich and poor.[2]

Liberation theology developed in the Third World. It was born of the unease that Christian theologians (mainly Roman Catholic) felt over the traditional interpretation of the gospel. Not all Christians accept it as a valid interpretation of the gospel.

Traditional theology can be described as two-world. There is the world of God and the world of human beings. Everything on earth is temporary, even a distraction from the things of God. People must put effort into a spiritual life of faith and prayer, for true riches are not in this world but outside it, beyond it, after it, in short in heaven. The poor will be rewarded when they die, if they have lived good, non-complaining lives, obeying the rules of the Church, for these are the official interpretation of God's will for people.

The liberation theologians in contrast see only one world. All that is known of God is known through human experience. God, the ground of all being, the reality in whom creation is rooted, is best understood in terms of love. God is seen most clearly in the life of the human Jesus. He was like a window through whom we see that God is loving and compassionate. That is why we call him God's own son. Whoever shows such Godlike love is also making God really present in the world. God, who created human beings 'in his own image', is tied down by his creation. People have the freedom to use their gifts for good or evil, and God cannot intervene by altering his laws to patch up mistakes. People are all called to make this one world grow towards its perfection. Poverty, injustice, greed and hatred prevent people from seeing God in his world, and distort God's plan. One-world theology calls upon Christians to take active, decisive moral stands in the world of politics and economics. (It is for this reason some Christians say it is a false response to the gospel. Jesus, after all, said 'My Kingdom is not of this world.')

A group of Christians from different church traditions and from seven different nations met in 1989 to explore their common Christian faith and moral obligation to the poor and oppressed peoples of the world. The resulting document, known as the 'Kairos Statement', outlines the new thinking among Christians and calls for a conversion of faith similar to the conversion experienced by Saul on the road to Damascus. Saul did a complete U-turn to become Paul the Christian missionary. The Kairos signatories appeal to the Churches: 'The time has come for a decisive turnabout on the part of those groups and individuals who have consciously or unconsciously compromised their Christian faith for political, economic or selfish reasons.'[3]

To whom is the document referring? Why, to the whole of the western world which for centuries has been growing richer at the expense of the Third World, and has fobbed off the exploited poor with its two-world theology of rewards in heaven. To the extent that the Churches have connived at such a policy, they convict themselves as guilty, and are called to conversion. The Kairos authors continue:

> The God whom the missionaries preached was a God who blessed the powerful, the conquerors, the colonisers. This God demanded resignation in the face of oppression . . . All that was offered to us by this God was an interior and other-worldly liberation . . . The Jesus who was preached to us was barely human. He seemed to float above history, above all human problems and conflicts. He condescended to make the poor the objects of his mercy, without sharing their oppression and their struggles. His death was a human sacrifice to placate an angry God. What was preached to us was a completely other-worldly Jesus who had no relevance to this life.

The document demands that we look at the Gospels afresh, and discover there a more liberating message. It encourages Christians whose lives are most oppressed to rethink their Christian faith, and to begin to take responsibility for their own liberation. Christians of El Salvador, Namibia and Korea have begun to rediscover God in the human Jesus and to speak of the Kingdom of God as the Rule of God, not in some other world but in this world completely transformed in accordance with God's plan. True, it stretches out beyond this life, but it begins in this life.

This renewed faith in the humanity of Jesus, and a recognition of God present in him and in the poor, has been adopted by many Christians in the West. It is known as taking 'a preferential option for the poor'. In recent years the Roman Catholic Church has made statements like the following: 'A preferential love should be shown to the poor who, as a consequence of their status, suffer oppression and powerlessness. Their needs and rights are given special attention in God's eyes.'

The Second Vatican Council, in a document *The Church in the Modern World*, admitted that the religious and secular world should be seen as one: 'There is no separation between the religious and the secular world. It is all God's; therefore faith and justice are linked together.'[4]

The new faith of the liberation Christians developed in two ways. Some Christians came to understand their faith as a commitment to the poor by actually going to live among them and sharing the oppression under which they live. Leading examples of such Christians are Sr Ita Ford, the murdered missionary nun in El Salvador; Dr Sheila Cassidy who went to Chile to offer her medical services to the oppressed; Fr Jon Sobrino the Spanish Jesuit missionary/theologian working in El Salvador; and Archbishop Desmond Tutu who is the voice for the black people in South Africa, oppressed under the apartheid system, which the Kairos statement describes as institutionalized and legalized racism.

For some Christians it worked the other way round. Active involvement with the poor came as a personal response to an imperative of faith, the fruit of prayerful reflection – especially in basic Christian communities.

From the beginning, the new development has caused grave concern among Church leaders. Many have viewed it with suspicion, and continue to do so seeing it as nothing other than a baptized form of Marxism. Pope John Paul II in particular has reservations about the liberation movement, and has been anxious to carpet a number of its most outstanding proponents. When he visited Peru in 1985, the Tupac Indians handed him a letter, expressing their sadness at such disapproval:

> We, the Indians of the Andes and America, have decided to take the opportunity of this visit by John Paul II to return to him his Bible. In five centuries, it has brought us neither love, nor peace, nor justice. Please take your Bible

> back, and return it to our oppressors. It is they, rather than we, who have need of its moral precepts.

The Indians and their liberation theology supporters clearly interpret gospel morality differently from the traditionalists.

One former traditionalist who eventually came to respect and embrace the new theology was Archbishop Oscar Romero of El Salvador. A Roman Catholic brought up in the traditional expression of Christianity and from a privileged background, Romero became, as Archbishop of San Salvador, a courageous defender of the poor against a corrupt government. Writing about him for CIIR, Jon Cortina SJ has no doubts about the validity of his approach:

> The first thing I want to say about Archbishop Romero is that he had a profound faith in God and that he believed in God as Jesus did. The measure of his faith . . . is the radical way in which he defended the cause of God. He did not make God's will something routine and trivial, as many Christians do, including priests and bishops. He did not restrict the will of God to a multitude of rules, the sort of ecclesiastical rules with which people now, as in the time of Jesus, seek to manipulate, belittle and even degrade God. Rather he sought the will of God where it is really to be found, where men and women are living and dying, where sin turns human beings into slaves and beasts of burden, and where the demand for justice and hope for a more human society is being forged.[5]

Archbishop Romero was killed because he became a voice for the poor. El Salvador has seen other Christian martyrs. One of them, Ignacio Ellacuria, a Jesuit priest killed in 1989, wrote of the moral obligation of Christians to stand on the side of the oppressed: 'Christians and all those who hate injustice are obliged to fight it with every ounce of their strength. They must work for a new world in which greed and selfishness will finally be overcome.'

This 'new world' was explored by the Latin American bishops

in the Conferences they held in Medellin in 1968, and in Pueblo in 1979. They analysed the role of the Church in the face of poverty and injustice, and concluded that the Church should cut its close links with the rich and powerful, and commit itself to seek new ways of being Christian, by making a 'fundamental option for the poor'. The bishops encouraged the participation of the people in their new vision by encouraging a restructuring of the Church in 'base Christian communities'. These are groups of ordinary people – mothers, students, labourers – who come together to share everyday experiences, and to work for change in the community, by group Bible study and prayer. These impoverished communities seek to change their society by bringing about justice, by overcoming greed, by challenging corrupt social, economic and political authority.

The base communities are criticized by traditional right-wing Christians as being subversive. The Kairos Christians have replied by accusing the traditionalists of a distorted belief which is equivalent to heresy:

> Right-wing Christianity replaces Christian responsibility and trust in God with submission to the yoke of slavery . . . The attempt to find security in blind obedience, absolute certainties and submission to authoritarianism is not faith. It is slavery. 'For freedom Christ has set us free; stand fast therefore, and do not submit again to the yoke of slavery' (Galatians 5:1, RSV).

Faith and moral behaviour cannot be separated. Shortly before his death Archbishop Romero explained his option for the poor in an address in Louvain:

> The course taken by the Archdiocese has clearly issued from its faith conviction. The transcendence of the gospel has guided us in our judgment and in our action. We have judged the social and political situation from the standpoint of the faith . . . As Church we are not political experts, nor do we want to engage in political manipulation. But entrance into the socio-political world, into the world where

the lives and deaths of the great mass of the population are decided, is necessary and urgent if we are to preserve, not only in word but in deed, faith in a God of life, and follow Jesus.

It will come as no surprise that the moral decisions taken by Archbishop Romero after his 'conversion' to liberation theology were somewhat different from what they were before. Faith and morality are closely linked. How people behave will depend deeply on what they believe.

On the other hand, reaching a moral decision is never easy or clear cut. The ethics of poverty and oppression for example is concerned to discover and then promote what is good for the poor. It is presumably good for the poor to have an adequate and balanced supply of food and to become self-reliant. But how do you define 'adequate'? What exactly is it to be self-reliant? What degree of non-reliance on others counts as self-reliance? On what do I rely for the answers I give to such questions? On what precise grounds do we make our moral decisions?

I had to take some sixth-formers through this topic recently for their A-level paper on ethics, and we needed to explore and tease out all the following categories.

1. There is first of all the *universal* value of an action. We call something good because everyone (or almost everyone) thinks something is good. In regard to justice for the poor, we could point to the 'universal' regard for human dignity enshrined in the 1948 United Nations Declaration of Human Rights. This is reinforced by the 1973 Humanist Manifesto for the Future which says 'The developed world has a moral obligation to assist the developing world.' However, this universal view is not foolproof. Majorities are not necessarily right.
2. Some Christians would tend to base morality on *natural law*, an approach introduced by Aristotle and developed by Thomas Aquinas. It is natural for people to have the will to live, so it is morally acceptable for the means to be taken to protect the lives of the oppressed. But this view also has

it a problems. Camilo Torres, a Colombian revolutionary priest, believed that terrorist activity, including killing, was an acceptable way to protect the lives of the poor in the struggle against unjust political regimes. Not everyone would agree with him.

3. Christians have often pointed to *conscience* as the ultimate guide to moral behaviour. It is considered as the voice of God. Newman, in response to the declaration of papal infallibility said, 'I shall drink to conscience first and to the pope second'. Psychology and sociology have, however, revealed that conscience is a highly complex thing. Long before Freud, theologians had to speak of an 'informed' conscience, that is to say, of the need to sensitize one's conscience so that it comes up with the correct results. Deception is always a possibility. Traditional Christians accuse liberation Christians of falling into this trap. They have been deceived into imagining that the gospel has to do with politics.
4. Base Christian communities will certainly be influenced by the 'teleological' argument, which considers the *good results* of an action. Good health, the reduction of misery and early death, the liberation of people to fulfil pursuits like learning and self-determination – all these give people a sense of dignity as God's children, made in his image. However, even this utilitarian argument, which looks for the greatest amount of good for the greatest number of people, still has its problems. When we in the North call for increased aid for the oppressed people of the South, bad effects can follow as well as good effects. The increased aid offered by the World Bank, for example, has served only to increase the poverty of the poorest nations, crippled now by a debt that can't even begin to be paid off. The money offered has even been used to produce nuclear arms, rather than to feed the people. Moral decisions which do not foresee all the consequences that could follow are fatally flawed.
5. Right-wing traditional Christians who challenge liberation morality might be more inclined to take the deontological stance of Kant, for whom end results are irrelevant.

Behaviour and choices must be based on the absolute *moral obligation* to act in accordance with reason. Traditional Christians tend to identify this sense of duty and absolute obligation with the moral code imposed by authority. Contraception is one of these absolutes. It is always totally wrong, and there are no circumstances imaginable in which it would be right. To introduce a population control programme using contraception in a poor country would always be wrong 'in itself'. The result of not introducing the programme (which may be thousands of deaths, malnutrition, disease and untold suffering) is outside the argument.

6. Such traditional Christians would certainly be very critical of any moral decision that was based on *situation ethics*. Joseph Fletcher in the 1960s was reacting against imposed Christianity when he developed a moral code which is based entirely on people's needs: 'The right thing to do is the most loving thing in any individual situation.' And this will obviously not be the same in every case. But is not a decision based on such a principle in danger of being a merely emotional one? This is certainly behind the reason why some Christians reject liberation theology. Indeed the situation ethics of the 1960s was condemned outright by Rome. And yet the liberationists have the Bible on their side. When Jesus tells the parable about the hungry being fed and the naked being clothed, what other ethic is he invoking but a situation ethic? Indeed, the Matthew 25 text, 'When I was hungry . . .' is not heard as a moral sermon by these Christians, but more as a total proclamation of the gospel. The Magnificat song which says, 'He has brought down the mighty from their thrones, and lifted up the lowly' (Luke 1:52), is seen as a revolutionary song calling all Christians to work for justice.

Conservative Christians who criticize liberation theology tend to find guidance for decision-making in the authority of their church tradition and government rather than in the Bible. It is not difficult to see how this has come about. The Christian way of life (morality) doesn't appear in the New Testament in the form of commandments and prohibitions. Joseph Fuchs SJ, commenting on the theologian Von Balthasar states clearly this position:

> Von Balthasar says quite rightly that our moral life should be measured by the person of Christ rather than by general laws . . . and that one's own being grounded on Christ is a more radical guide than universal norms. Therefore, he calls Christ the most concrete norm, because he is an individual person, and at the same time the most universal norm, because he is the measure of each and every person and of every situation.[6]

When liberation Christians look at Jesus, they recognize his humanity. They see that Jesus was obedient to the moral claim – as he saw it – by making personal decisions as each situation demanded. He sought to discover the kind of world God had in mind and he made every effort to bring it about. This brought him to his death as a martyr.

It is interesting that Frank Turner, an English Jesuit, describes an incident in the Gospel where this human Jesus nearly makes a bad moral choice. He reflects on the story of the Syro-Phoenician woman, who like hungry, oppressed people everywhere, begs Jesus for food: 'Here in this story, and perhaps only here, he appears as the one with privilege, the one who himself needs to be challenged . . . Daringly, Mark's Gospel here presents Jesus as grudging, even hostile.'[7]

The writer concludes that Jesus, like us, is formed and taught by others, and in this case, by the most unlikely person, the outsider, the poor. He goes on to say that the Church's 'option for the poor' should be influenced by this episode. The choice is not merely to raise the standard of life for the poor, it is much more fundamental. It is a need, a recognition that the Church 'must allow itself to be decisively influenced by the experience of the poor. A faithful response to this call would transform Church life in ways we can hardly anticipate.' He is describing a situationist and liberationist view of the Church.

It is time this chapter was brought to an end. Has liberation theology introduced a new maturity into the Church? Who knows? Christians who interpret their religion in a heteronomous way will continue to develop their moral values in close dependence upon church authority. Some Roman Catholics, for example, will look to the Pope to tell them if liberation theology is a valid interpretation of the gospel. He will be very cautious in his response.

Theonomous Christians will feel free to make up their own minds, using conscience, reason and their own understanding of the Bible. For these Christians, ethics is made up not of general principles but of challenges to which people are invited to respond. Such Christians will surely feel 'at home' with liberation theology, as will all Christians who feel stifled by the more authoritarian two-world view.

Resolutions for the class-room

***First idea** (for 12-year-olds)*

Outside my classroom we have painted a large tree on the wall. It is a permanent background for display work, and it makes an excellent base for my Pentecost Tree. We talk about the fruits of the Holy Spirit when we discuss the sacrament of confirmation, and the younger children like to make apple and pear shapes on which they write their own descriptions of the Pauline list of fruits. I developed this idea recently in a more interesting way. I got one class to make dozens of leaves to put on our tree and on each one they wrote about one person who, in their estimation, is full of the Spirit of love. There were some fine tributes to family and friends. One boy wrote on his leaf: 'My Mum is full of the spirit of patience and goodness because she goes on and on looking after us even when we grumble and argue.' Jane wrote a rather unexpected tribute: 'My dentist has the spirit of joy. It is quite a pleasure to go to him because he makes me laugh.'

With my next class I will suggest we look for outstanding people who have witnessed their Christianity to the world: Archbishop Romero, Sheila Cassidy, Fr Damien, Jackie Pullinger, for example. Their portraits will decorate our tree as we look at the gospel orientation of their lives.

***Second idea** (for 13-year-olds)*

I want to make some banners and an altar frontal to use during school liturgies, especially for feast days. It would be interesting to explore the theme of the Holy Spirit in the Bible and then ask groups of pupils to illustrate the stories and references in colourful and symbolic ways. We will choose the most successful results and transfer the designs onto material. I can imagine bright and interesting shapes, representing wind, fire and water.

Third idea

Whenever I ask a class about the Holy Spirit they usually speak of the dove, referring to the gospel description of Jesus' baptism in the Jordan, when God's Spirit, dove-like, descended upon him. I would like to explore this symbol of the gentle, peaceful presence of the Holy Spirit with older students. It is always a temptation with examination classes to press on with syllabus material without pausing for some deep, personal reflection. Without it they have little chance to mature and grow in faith. On one of our off-site reflection days with the 15-year-olds I will take 'Peace' as our theme. Peter de Rosa has a prayer about the Spirit of peace that I will use as a source of our meditation.

> Father, at the Supper, Jesus said: Peace I leave with you;
> my peace I give to you;
> not as the world gives do I give to you.
> The peace Christ left with us, Father,
> is the peace of the Dove,
> the gentle presence of the Holy Spirit.
> In Christ you blessed your people with peace,
> because in him we find the Spirit
> of love and reconciliation.
> Over the troubled waters of his disciples' hearts,
> the risen Christ said, 'Peace, be still!'
> and the winds fell and the waves ceased

and at last they found themselves to be men of peace.
Whatever tribulations they had in the world,
in Christ they had peace,
for he had overcome the world.
The risen Christ breathed on them;
and borne upon his breath
was the Dove of your divine forgiveness:
and they blessed you, Father, for your grace and peace.
Father, may the Whitsuntide Christ
breathe his Spirit of peace on me.
Make me worthy to be called your child
by making me an instrument of your peace.
In the Holy Spirit, Father,
I have calmed and quieted my soul
like a child quieted at its mother's breast;
like a child that is quieted is my soul.[8]

One practical part of the day would be a task set for the participants to select slides (from the hundreds we have collected over the years) to accompany a public reading of the prayer. We would also make a 'graffiti wall' where each student is asked to paint on a prepared wall a sentence beginning 'Peace is . . .'.

5

BY WHOSE AUTHORITY?

Jesus comes to his friends
when they are helped by their ministers
to worship God in an orderly way.

I recently attended my priest-cousin's silver jubilee celebration Mass. I was delighted to discover the warmth and genuine affection of hundreds of past and present parishioners for Fr Bill. I was most impressed that neither he, nor the preacher, nor his bishop spoke long and heavy words about the great gift of priesthood. As a result what emerged was gratitude for a man who has put his life at the service of people. Bill's fellow priests, dozens of them, remained quietly at the side of the church for most of the celebration. Bill's parishioners, former parishioners, family and friends were the most prominent. I felt very comfortable and happy taking part in this family and church celebration.

By contrast, I felt uneasy and dissatisfied earlier this year at the Holy Week diocesan Mass for the blessing of oils at our cathedral-parish church. At this celebration dozens of priests surrounded the bishop and took centre stage, as he praised them for their fidelity to the great vocation of holy orders. It was a visual and aural bombardment of our senses: this was the Church in all its power and authority and maleness. Of course, I didn't always feel this way. I grew up in admiration of the immense power of church leadership. It was impressed upon us, as children, that the Pope, bishops and priests had a very special relationship to God which resulted in their having a deeper knowledge of God than we could ever achieve; and they were given power and authority over all lay members of the Church whose role, as subjects, was simply to obey without question. There was something safe and secure about this. I remember my immense pride at Easter time when the Pope sent his blessing, *Urbi et Orbi*, out across the packed St Peter's Square. He was always flanked by bishops and priests and the sight was enough to confirm my willing submission to a patriarchal church.

I was recently in Rome and quite surprised myself that I had not the slightest inclination to attend a church celebration which was presided over by the Pope. At a previous visit, nearly thirty years before, I had clapped and cheered and jostled in the crowd in an attempt to get near to Pope Paul VI. But this time I felt different, far more detached. Rome had lost none of its charm – the history, the art, the city of early Christian and medieval faith. But the overpowering majesty of St Peter's was oppressive for it spoke of authority, subjection and aggrandizement. The daily stream of black-frocked seminarians hurrying from the Gregorian University, clutching their leather briefcases, seemed to be in training to become the daily stream of black suited, solemn-faced prelates, clutching their expensive leather briefcases, who made their way to and from the Vatican. It was quite enough to convince me that my model of church has changed dramatically.

Over the centuries the role of the priest became so important that priests were regarded as the true representatives of God and of the Church. When Bert, my husband, withdrew from the priesthood, newspaper reporters quite naturally wrote that he had 'left the Church'. He would certainly argue that he had, in fact, just joined the real Church. For he himself wrote in a children's book on the sacraments: 'No group of Jesus' friends can claim to be "in charge" of the Church. Less still any one single Christian. All the friends of Jesus, together, make up the Church. The teachings of Jesus, and the sacraments, belong to all of them, not to any one person or group.' In this same booklet Bert goes on to describe the Sacrament of Order as the means by which the Christian family can grow in an orderly way and learn to follow Jesus' way of the cross. He concludes – with considerable feeling – 'When the ministers themselves set the example, this sacrament can bring Jesus very close to his friends.'

It is no easy task to convince my students of the value of the priesthood. By and large, together with other adolescents, most of them are simply not interested in a way of life which suggests that human sexuality is a hindrance to union with God and to the service of others. Many of them do not actually know any priest who sets them a role model, or who puts them in mind of Jesus the Servant. For many of the pupils have stopped attending church, perhaps just to assert their independence, but in some cases because their families have suffered from an over-authoritarian priest. Others attend parishes where the priest happens to be an uninspiring preacher or a simple embarrassment by his total inability to relate to other human beings. A few are finally disenchanted by the recent popular press images of priests or bishops unfaithful to their celibacy or even responsible for sexual abuse of children.

So it takes a great deal of effort and self-discipline on my part, as a teacher, to offer my pupils some understanding and appreciation of the priestly, male, celibate life which is the practice in my Church. The best chance of success I have is to introduce lively, warm, intelligent and open-minded priests to the pupils. Thank God they do exist, but I have to say that most of the Catholic teachers I know live in apprehension about the bishop's choice of school chaplain. It is he who is going to influence the young in their practical view of the local Church. The responsibility on him is enormous. One wrong step, one miscalculated intrusion into their lives, and they could be alienated from the Church for ever. On the other hand, a kindly, sympathetic, loving ear can have the opposite effect. I recall the experience of Anthony Bloom, the Russian Archbishop who lives in London. His most formative experience in his faith journey was a priest he met at a boys' summer camp when he was an 11-year-old atheist. He was struck by the priest's warmth and love, by the way he responded to everyone without conditions or favouritism. Later on, when the future archbishop read the gospel and discovered the compelling person of Jesus, he began to understand what he had recognized but could not name in the priest. He calls that first meeting – not the reading of the gospel – his 'first deep spiritual experience'.

I noticed only last week, as I read my parish weekly newsletter, how I have shifted the emphasis in my teaching on this sacrament. Our parish priest had written an article asking us to be aware of the great generosity of two people, a young man who was to be ordained priest the following Sunday and a young woman who had taken final vows at the local Carmelite monastery that week. In a second paragraph he mentioned that, of course, married people have an important vocation too. The priest writing this article is a personal friend and one of the first whom I invite into my class-room. He, by his enthusiasm, his humour and his humanity does indeed inspire young people to look twice at the Church. But even he, probably inevitably, puts marriage into a 'second paragraph'. It suggests an afterthought. I realized how I've changed since my childhood. I no longer want to isolate the sacrament of orders, or the vocation to the religious life, from the married or single state. I simply want to present to my students the Christian ideal of choosing to live according to the gospel Jesus – a life of generosity, selflessness and service of others. I then point out that it is incidental how we choose, or feel 'called', to live this out. It may be as a wife and mother; it may be as a priest serving a large group of Christians; it may be as a single person devoted to a parent or pursuing a career of service to the wider community; or it may be as a professed member of a religious community. What matters, I point out, is the degree of love and selflessness brought to others, not the choice of vocation. Had I been Fr John, my parish priest, I would have written something like this in the weekly bulletin:

> We remember with prayerful congratulations this week all those who are starting out on new journeys of faith and commitment. We remember especially Jane and Robert who are to be married on Saturday; Maureen who took her final vows at Mount St Mary's; Erica who starts her nursing training shortly, and James who is to be ordained deacon

next week. We pray that they follow the example of Jesus in serving others with generosity, love and humour.

Only when I have established this idea of vocation can I get down to demonstrating the role of a priest – as I see it. I suffered enormously in the past from disillusionment because of the false teaching I had been given. We were led to believe that the priesthood – and, for us girls, the religious life – was the better choice, the chance actually to follow in the footsteps of Jesus, the celibate Holy One of God. In brief, if we wanted holiness we really had to leave behind the distractions of the world and enter into a spiritual world of total dedication where holiness was possible. Such exhortation led me to believe firstly that in priests I would always recognize the most faithful followers of the gospel, and, secondly, that I would find the most God-like companions only in the convent. Experience has shown me that this is patently untrue. I have learnt not without disappointment and grief along the road, that holiness has all to do with wholeness, and wholeness is exactly what some nuns and priests never achieve. I must point out, of course, that some do.

I don't want my teaching to be negative and critical so I try to be absolutely neutral. I have developed a way of presenting the priestly vocation in the context of authority and organization in the Church. No one can argue with the witness of the past, so we take a look at church history to try and discover the role of the priest in the past and in the present. We start of course with the Gospels, and notice that the texts all speak of humility and service. 'Call no one rabbi, or master or father, or papa or pope. The greatest amongst you must be your servant' (own translation of Matthew 23:9). Mark says that Jesus warned of those who wear long clothes, are greeted in public, sit at the top table and are known as professional holy people (Mark 12:38). These are difficult texts to read and digest when you have just seen on the television news the Archbishop of Canterbury, in full robes, in a banquet hall with the royal family.

Jesus seems to have had rather radical ideas about leadership and authority. It had little in common with authority understood in the usual order of things: kings, governments or police. The most important and authoritative people amongst his followers would be those with no power, like children. These would recognize that all authority must be based on love, and as such would always be expressed in the unostentatious service of others.

My pupils and I have to admit that the Church, in all its branches, has not measured up well to these ideals of Jesus. The simple brotherly service that a group of twelve or thirteen can do towards each other is no longer possible when the group grows into thousands: even St Paul found that in New Testament times. And what do you do when the thousands become millions, and the group has turned into an institution, 'Church plc'?

The origins of the priesthood lie in the New Testament itself. The writing known as the Letter to the Hebrews highlights the characteristics of the ministry of Jesus: his humanity, his compassion and his fidelity. It concludes that Jesus is a priest for ever, interceding for us all before God: 'This one, because he remains for ever, can never lose his priesthood. It follows, then, that his power to save is utterly certain, since he is living for ever to intercede for all who come to God through him' (Hebrews 7:25, JB).

Peter, in his first letter, points out that this one priesthood of Jesus has now devolved on to the whole community. The fundamental truth of Christianity is that all believers, through their baptism, are commissioned to proclaim the Good News of the gospel, by entering into the one priesthood of Jesus: 'You are a chosen race, a royal priesthood, a consecrated nation, a people set apart to sing the praises of God who called you out of darkness into his wonderful light' (1 Peter 2:9, JB).

Everyone therefore, without exception, has the responsibility for building up the body of Christ and sharing in its mission. Within the body of Christ there are no 'honorary members'. But I can hear my pupils say, 'Well, it doesn't seem like that. What about the Pope and the cardinals and all the pomp and ceremony that surrounds them?'

The need for leadership within the body of the Church was always there. It was only natural that the apostles, with Peter as spokesman, assumed that role in the beginning. As the communities grew and the work of the Church increased, it was obviously necessary for new leaders to emerge, with differing roles. So Paul and Barnabas appointed 'elders', and other overseers of the churches were called 'episcopoi'. Assistants to the new leaders were called 'deacons', with Stephen and Philip being the most well known.

When I was exploring the Acts of the Apostles and Paul's letters with some Year-9 pupils in this way, one of them asked me, 'How do women priests fit into all this?' Another commented, 'How come that we have no married priests in our church, when Paul tells Titus to pick elders who have stable marriages and well-behaved children?' This left me with the problem of explaining the diminishing role of lay people (who used to choose their own bishops and play an important role in Synods and Councils), and the gradual emergence over the centuries of an almost exclusively clerical leadership. I point out that by the end of the fifth century the bishops and priests began to enjoy a status equivalent to their political counterparts. They even began to dress in a distinct way (obviously ignoring Mark 12:36!). It was the beginning of a clerical privilege which separated the clergy from the laity. It has taken another fifteen centuries for the Church to re-examine this distinction, and to try and reinstate the New Testament ideal of one Body, one People of God, with no second-class citizens.

I answer the two girls' questions first by quoting theologians like John Wilkinson, who writes:

> We are only just beginning to realise the many gifts that are available in the Church and that have not been tapped. We have yet to benefit from many new forms of ministry and service, especially from women who for too long have been excluded from so many effective forms of ministry.[1]

In the discussion that follows it takes very little time for the students themselves to point out that it was obvious no woman would be appointed a leader in those days of the early Church, given the secondary role that all women had to accept in first-century male-dominated society. I point out that Jesus' attitude to women (according to Luke) made him something of an exception. He happily broke free from accepted and expected behaviour in order to treat women on equal terms to men. Members of the Anglican faith reading these pages may be interested to know that, as far as I can tell, the vast majority of our young Roman Catholics welcome the idea of women priests. Indeed many of them are totally disenchanted with the Churches for making such a fuss about this particular issue when, as they say, 'The world is crying out for compassion and caring in the midst of wars, famine and endless suffering, and all we hear about is arguments over women priests or married priests.'

Which brings me to the second girl's question about celibacy. I point out first of all, that it is only in the Roman Catholic branch of the Western Church that celibacy is a requirement for both priests and bishops. The custom of celibacy was introduced in the fourth century as a voluntary, but recommended practice. The tradition was only imposed on all the clergy in AD 1139. The idea behind the rule of celibacy is that it enables the priest to be free for the total service of his community and is intended to enrich the possibilities of giving and receiving friendship with everyone he meets, men and women, married and single, young and old.

In the discussion that follows I have a difficult time supporting the official line because the objections come fast and furious at me. The usual arguments appear: how can an unmarried man possibly speak with authority and understanding on matters concerning marriage or family issues, especially on birth control? I answer this one by inviting into school a priest, hand-picked, whom I know as an energetic, loving, laughing, pastoral man with a gift of communication with the young. He convinces them. Mind you he is a most unusual priest, who enables many marginalized Catholics to remain in the Church who would otherwise find themselves alienated.

The most recent objections put up by my pupils are more difficult to answer. I cannot, myself, see any way to support the present Roman Catholic practice of continuing to require celibacy from Catholic priests whilst encouraging married Anglican priests to move across denominations and become married Catholic priests. 'Well,' said one boy, 'if I thought of becoming a priest I would simply become an Anglican, get ordained and married, then join up with the Catholic Church again. Mind you, it won't happen. All this is such a nonsense that I'd never become a priest anyway.'

How am I expected to answer that? Perhaps the anomaly of the present situation will force the Catholic Church to rethink its policy on obligatory celibacy. I have no doubt that there are many individuals, perhaps natural bachelors anyway, who live with their celibacy in an honest and generous way. I admire their self-sacrifice and warmly point out to my pupils the example and selfless care for others these priests have.

But my private thoughts on the matter I have to hold back from the classroom. I am seriously disheartened and sometimes angry at the hypocrisy I have witnessed in my Church's attitude to and protection of its priests.

The law of obligatory celibacy has caused immense harm to individuals within and without the priesthood. For centuries the law has meant that young ordained men have been forced to live as a 'monk in his own monastery'. Monastic life is one thing: a high ideal where heroic individuals have pursued holiness and witnessed to the importance of the Kingdom of God; a refuge for some hurt individuals who cannot cope with the rigours of day-by-day human relationships or who are terrified of sexuality; a safer haven than our prejudiced society for some individuals with homosexual orientation. But a lonely person is different from the person who can live alone. I suspect there are very few of the latter and they are the only ones capable of living a celibate life without the danger of damaging their personalities.

Loneliness leads some priests to hurt themselves and others. I think of the number of Catholic priests I know, or have known, who became alcoholic in an understandable drift into compensatory drinking. Only twice in my life have I sat embarrassed and uncomfortable in the presence of someone whose speech was slurred and behaviour unpredictable. Both times the drunken men were priests.

Enforced celibacy is today even being blamed (whether rightly or wrongly) for homosexual liaisons amongst the clergy and the horrific revelations only now emerging of the many cases of child sexual abuse in religious institutions. I presume the priests involved entered the ordained priesthood in order, genuinely, to seek a way of life that would control their natural sexual orientation, or, in the case of abuse, their sexual disorder. But what is absolutely infuriating and unjust is the church authority's inability to be honest about the situation. Hypocrisy is now a word I find creeping more regularly into my vocabulary. What has happened to the Christian community over the centuries that it has felt compelled to hide its human failings and refuse to come clean about the difficulties its priest-members have to face? It wasn't so in the early Church. Paul, in his letters, and Luke in the Acts of the Apostles, are quite open about the problems and failures of the growing communities. It was later generations of Christians who white-washed the situation, and presented an idyllic early Church where everyone loved and cared for each other and shared all they had. It was clearly not like that. I get angry today when bishops – the Pope included – talk as though the priests have always been a race apart, holy and selfless all the time, wonderful images of the Son of God. It is actually unfair to the priests themselves, who as human beings cannot live up to the ideal of holiness all the time.

Celibacy is certainly one ideal that many priests cannot live up to. It is in this respect that I feel most distress. I know a good number of honest men who left the priesthood in order to get married. They did so when they recognized that they found it impossible to obey the celibacy rule. They left with integrity. Some men, now happily married, would give anything to resume their vocation to priestly service of the community; some have never found work that fulfils their need to work with people. But they are not acceptable to the Pope or the bishops. Indeed in some cases they are made to feel outcasts and failures in the

Church. (They should of course, as my student suggested, have become Anglicans early on!)

At the same time I know a number of priests who are also unable to keep their rule of celibacy, but have stayed. I presume their bishops are also aware of the problem (perhaps some even share it). I am outraged that they satisfy their sexual needs by liaisons with parishioners, married or single, whilst still presenting to the community the Church's teaching that sexual intercourse outside marriage is wrong and that adultery is a sin. Presumably they also need to practise contraception to keep their relationship a secret. My argument here is not with the moral teaching of the Church (which I discuss in the next chapter), but with the two-faced hypocrisy of the priests concerned. I am most distressed at the disregard for women used in this way. They have to remain the silent, suffering victims of the priests' needs. Of course it takes two to make the relationship, but her needs have always to give way to his desire to remain publicly acceptable to the Church. If the woman becomes pregnant she can be treated with disregard and, as the case of Annie Murphy and the Bishop of Galway showed us recently, with a certain cruelty.

I detected in the story of Annie Murphy as well as in other stories of liaisons between priest and parishioner, a certain arrogance on the part of the priests. They must be considered and protected at all costs, no matter what pain it caused to their partner. I think it is this that worries me most about the rule of celibacy for non-monastic ordained men. The lone man can become desperately selfish. He doesn't need to give way to others, to be tempered in his attitudes by other people's needs. The married man has to give and take within his marriage, or he becomes a monster. The lone man can become totally unrealistic about his life-style. I always smile when the priest is unavailable because he has to take his day off, religiously, week by week. What father of a family ever has a day off when he can do precisely his 'own thing'? He usually exchanges the work in the office or factory for mending the dripping tap, painting the hallway, chauffeuring the children here and there, or doing his share of the home-making. I remember being horrified years ago, on a visit to Canada, being shown around the luxury, ranch-like house and extensive grounds which a priest was building for his own retirement. It was rather far removed from the possibilities open to most of the families in his parish, let alone to the gospel Jesus whom he purported to follow.

Perhaps the greatest problem all along, in our Catholic tradition, has been the failure for centuries to read the gospel accurately. I am looking for some reason why our typical priest seems to have strayed so far from the life Jesus led. Perhaps I have glimpsed a reason in a footnote written in a book prepared for teachers by Fr Paddy Purnell SJ, *Our Faith Story*:

> My entry into the religious life (Society of Jesus) re-inforced the image of God I had built for myself. Along with all forms of religious life at that time, the Jesuits were authoritarian and they specialised in obedience. If my memory serves me well, we were never directly encouraged to read the bible, nor even the new testament; whereas time was specifically allocated to certain spiritual writers renowned for their views on religious obedience.[2]

Hardly surprising then if the role of priest emerged in total contrast to the gospel Jesus who came to serve, and who lived in poverty, even to burial in a borrowed grave.

Over the centuries the role of the priest changed from a ministry of service within the local community to a performer of sacred rites, centred around the Mass. The rite of ordination underwent significant changes over the centuries, and by the Middle Ages it implied that priesthood was the only effective source of ministry in the Church. Ordination conferred a power, the power to consecrate and offer the Eucharist. All other ministries that existed amongst the laity were seen as essential steps on the way to priesthood. That cut women out altogether! All this had a profound effect on the shape and style of the liturgy. The laity became spectators; priests spoke about 'my Mass' and 'my Parish'.

This idea of the priesthood, which gives the priest power over the people, is still with us. It is far removed from the ministry described by Paul in the first century. Ministers of the word abound in those early writings, in fact Paul expects all Christians to speak out for Christ. But he says absolutely nothing about a minister of the Eucharist. We are told that the Eucharist was celebrated at Corinth, but although he makes some harsh criticisms, he does not address a minister or talk of a priest in charge. The theologian Schillebeeckx has, I believe, made a most important contribution to the debate about ministry, by pointing out that lay people were probably the first ministers of the sacrament:

> For the New Testament there is evidently no special problem to who should preside at the eucharist; we are told nothing directly in this connection . . . The general conception is that anyone who is competent to lead the community in one way or another is *ipso facto* also president of the eucharist.

Schillebeeckx was, of course, much criticized for making this observation and concluding from it that lay people could preside at their own Eucharists. But I strongly suspect that in the future the Churches will follow this line. I sincerely hope so.

The reforms of Vatican II opened up the way to a deeper respect for lay ministry among Catholics, and the courageous step taken by the Church of England Synod to ordain women as priests has prepared the way for a revision of the idea of priestly vocation and ordination. We are living in the time of rapid change when the practice of centuries is being challenged. Change will have to come quickly because of the shortage of applicants to the priesthood, and because our young church members see very little involvement for them as things stand at present.

A recent event at my school caused me and other teachers great distress as it revealed just how difficult it is for young people to be accepted in our churches. A group of sixth-formers went away for a residential retreat, and were accompanied by teachers and a priest. They had a wonderful experience of sharing, of prayer, of listening to one another and of exploring their faith. They were invited by the retreat team (Teaching Brothers) to prepare the liturgy and offer their reflections at the time of the sermon. For them it was a profound experience, a Mass which lasted two hours and allowed them to feel (some for the first time) that it was their liturgy. They spoke about it for many weeks later. But the priest was outraged, angry, bewildered that his preaching role was usurped by the laity. He has refused to accompany other young people to another such retreat experience because it left him feeling 'not in charge' (his words).

The tragedy is that this priest is well liked and appreciated by young people, and he had only been ordained three years. What kind of training are they still having in the seminary? I have to ask myself if anything has really changed since Vatican II? I would have to support my students if they refused to attend this priest's 'own' Masses, and preferred to celebrate in their own way. That didn't happen, the sixth-formers were courteous and generous, and continued to attend school Masses, but I suspect with little heart.

I have heard complaints from parishioners that few of our young people are seen regularly at church, in spite of the open doors and great welcome offered them. 'Look at our flower festival this year,' one lady said to me, 'it was a wonderful and successful way of attracting people. But I didn't see many teenagers there.' My reaction was, Thank God you didn't, because the theme of 'Glory to God' was developed in such a way as to alienate them even further. The flower displays in every corner of the cathedral were exquisite. But I don't think 15-year-olds would be very impressed by seeing the all-blue display, with leather handbag, representing 'Mrs Thatcher, Glory in Achievement'; less still by the all-white display with a tennis racket called 'Fred Perry and Virginia Wade, Glory in Sport'. The display representing the Glory of Youth was an old annual (*Beano*, I think), and a Guide uniform with neat rows of badges! And I could hardly believe my eyes when I saw our bishop's throne in the apse draped with a rich red velvet cloth and entitled 'The Glory of the Empire'.

At the back of the cathedral, a delightful table had been decorated with small arrangements of delicate and exotic flowers, representing nations of the world. A fellow parishioner whispered to me, 'Odd to see such beautiful displays representing Third-World countries which aren't beautiful at all – in all their poverty.' I noticed at that moment that, in order to make room for the table, our permanent display showing pictures of our twinned parish in Peru had been removed. Our struggling brothers and sisters had been tidily relegated out of sight, and locked in the sacristy. At that moment I thought of an idea for a school class.

On Monday morning I gave out to my 12-year-olds an outline plan of a church on A3 paper. I gave them the theme 'The Glory of God', and told them to work in pairs and plan a flower festival for their church. They needed to select about fifteen spots to place their displays, giving them a name and describing (or drawing on additional paper) the displays in detail. I was not disappointed by the response, in fact some designs moved me deeply. Nearly every pair chose an overall theme of 'Love' – the Glory of God shown when people care about one another. There were displays for Mother Teresa in blue and white, for parents who 'care about us', for organizations like Christian Aid and CAFOD, and for more general caring groups like nurses and social workers. But what impressed me most of all was the sense of reality which these 12-year-olds were able to convey, and which was so sadly missing in the adults' presentation. Some flowers, for example, were drawn and annotated 'dye black to show death and misery'. One pair of boys even asked me if they could include stands of dead and dying flowers to represent the situation in war-torn countries: 'We will then put one living flower amongst them to show the sign of hope.'

When children produce work like this, the weary RE teacher revives and is given heart to keep on going. In other words she is ministered to by her pupils. This is the shared ministry which I want to see recognized and authenticated in our Christian communities today. I firmly believe that there needs to be a radical change in the nature of priestly ministry. We minister to one another in our daily lives and, as baptized Christians, we relate this to the life of Jesus, and recognize that it is this loving service of one another that enables us to become whole and happy people. The priestly ministry is an important one but no more so than any other. It assumes importance over all other ministries because of the unwieldly parish system of community which is an artificial grouping of people. The parish is usually too large to express what community really means, and needs an administrator, an organizer, a 'wonder-worker' to keep so many different groups of people happy! In addition we hand over to him the liturgy, the sick visiting, the counselling, the marriage guidance. Any wonder that our poor priests can crack up, or think they alone have all the answers. We make them think they have.

Our churches are aware of the problems and have attempted to rectify the over-importance given to the one man in charge. In the Catholic tradition he is assisted today by Eucharistic Ministers and Lay-Readers. Some parishes have appointed permanent married deacons, but when they choose to wear dog-collars they have simply joined the hierarchy and again emphasized the clerical–lay divide. This doesn't inspire me with hope. But then neither does the sight of Anglican women deacons or Methodist women ministers wearing clerical collars. Why do they need to copy the men? Why put on a piece of plastic and a grey bib to announce their position? Is the ordination of women going to turn out to be no more than the upping of another group of church members as the 'professional Christians', one step above the rest?

I must sound disheartened. Perhaps I am, but only with the situation in the weary Western world. My doubts turned to near despair only a few years ago when I saw the outcome of our Diocesan Lay Conference, hailed as a great step forward in giving a voice to the people. The published report from the conference, drawn up after the event by a priest of course, produced the model for a diocesan church structure displayed opposite. Is it any wonder that the people of God can feel crushed by the sheer weight of a hierarchically structured church? The laity lie at the bottom of the pile.

But I am not disheartened by the other model of the Church, which I referred to in a previous chapter (see pages 37–8). The base communities, in what we call the Third-World countries,

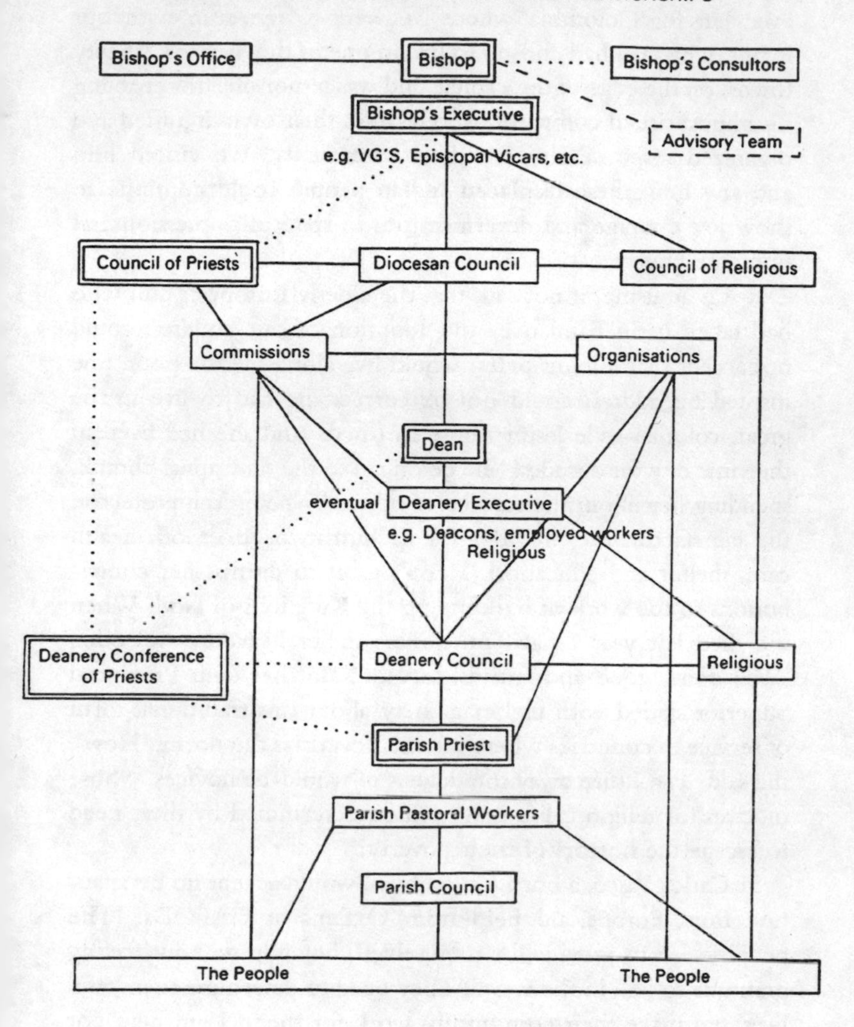

are giving us a new insight into how the Church can return to New Testament values and thereby give hope for survival in the future. We had a brief encounter with a base community and the role of an ordained priest in this setting when we went to Colombia to adopt our children. We had heard of Carlos Vasco, a Jesuit mathematics lecturer at Bogotá University, before we even left for Colombia where we were to meet up with our infant twins. He had chosen to live in one of the 'barrios' (shanty towns) on the edge of the capital, and was responsible for enabling his impoverished companions to take on their own dignified and organized responsibility for their community. We visited him and saw how these displaced Indian people could continue to show joy, courage and determination in spite of oppression and immense poverty.

It was amusing, if not sad, that the elderly European nun who had taken us in hand over the adoption of our children could not accept that a Jesuit priest would live alongside the poor. She insisted his address could not be correct; he had to live in the great, colonial-style Jesuit house in town. And she had lived in the same city for decades! She belonged to the traditional church, spending her life in the service of others by being the protector, the benefactor, the provider for all human needs; food, health care, shelter and education. I don't want to dismiss her contributions to the work of building up the Kingdom of God. When she died last year I have no doubt of her heavenly welcome, 'Well done, good and faithful servant'. But her own Provincial Superior shared with us her anxiety about this traditional form of service in countries where intense poverty is the norm. 'How', she said, 'can I turn away the dozens of would-be novices, whose motives for religious life may well be determined by their need to escape the horrors of their poverty?'

Fr Carlos Vasco, a born Colombian, would accept no benefaction from Europe, no help from Oxfams or CAFODs: 'The people need to provide for themselves', he said, 'without feeling gratitude to you in the west.' 'They need to determine their own lives and make their community work for them. I am here not to tell them what to do, or to preach at them, but to listen, to offer ideas if they ask, celebrate a liturgy if they want, and point them in the right direction for help on matters they have no experience in.'

The first thing his community did was build a school-room where their Bible-based meetings could also take place. Fr Carlos told us that his presence with the poor had aroused attention and criticism from both Church and political leaders. He had in fact been imprisoned for supporting the people: the communists were active in Colombia and accused him of not helping the people by being too much involved with the establishment, and the Church officials suspected him of being 'left' or Marxist. 'If I can't please either group, perhaps I have got it about right', he said. The obvious contentment and generous sharing between family and family that we witnessed made us feel that he had indeed got it right.

One of the most helpful books I have recently read about the base communities is the Christian Aid Lent book for 1993, *Celebrating Resistance*, written by Dorothee Soelle, translated by Joyce Irwin. She describes with an economy of words (that I admire) the *pueblos jovenes* – 'young towns' or slums in Peru. These communities, huddled together on the outskirts of the town surprised Dorothee by their cleanliness and order. She discovered the organized self-help of the poor.

> The reputation of persons in these settlements is not determined by their attitude toward money but by their sense of responsibility for the whole. The delegates who wait for hours outside government offices are highly respected. They usually cannot organize meetings before ten in the evening. Many women live with the threefold burden of jobs, caring for home and children and work in the base organization. In one Bible-study group the women said in response to the question of what sin is: 'Whoever does not go to the common meeting and excludes himself from the community is in sin'![3]

From these communities of the laity a new discovery of the gospel is emerging, and hence a new theology. The communities will not be perfect and the theology will be inevitably flawed as theologies always are. There is a danger, as the author of this book points out, that liberation theology will become just one more theoretical treatise to be studied in the seminaries and divinity schools, alongside the other volumes of Church Dogmatics. Some people already suggest that base communities are on the decline because other forces than the Church are coming to the aid of the dispossessed, or because new appointments of reactionary bishops are suppressing this movement of the people. Dorothee Soelle challenges this view because she has witnessed the strength of the ordinary people, especially the women who are the most natural leaders of the communities. (The world recognized this by awarding one such woman, Rigoberto Menches, the Nobel Peace Prize earlier this year.) The fact is, according to Dorothee, 'the more conservative the Roman politics of the Vatican, the more strength flows into the lay movement'. The people themselves are evaluating the role of the clergy in their lives. This movement 'is indestructible' writes one Mexican Indian. 'Bishops can be replaced, training centres can be closed, but they cannot get rid of the people. Ultimately the people sustain the Church. Dependence on priests is a basic mistake of the Churches in the West.'

I sincerely hope that from this new theology and experience of the people will come a fresh idea of priesthood which will eventually be experienced in our continent too. A new model will never work if it is discussed and analysed in endless workshops, committees, Synods or Councils as a prelude to being imposed from the top. It will come quietly, and arise inevitably out of the experience of ordinary people who move under the guidance of the Holy Spirit, wherever they work for the human good of one another.

Resolutions for the class-room

First idea

I must encourage my students to think through the way communities need some organization and leadership. So I will create a form of role-play for the 16-year-olds. I will set the scene in the first century. All the group has to go on is the memory and influence of Jesus, whose life I will outline; including his concern for 'marginal' people, his capacity to forgive, his last supper with the command to 'do this in memory of me', his teaching on prayer, his death and the resurrection experience of Peter and the women.

The task is to decide how their community (the whole class) should live their lives as followers of Jesus. I would leave them alone for 30 minutes with no advice about organizing the time and interpreting the task. On my return I will de-brief the group on two levels; first how they actually set about organizing the lesson and secondly what conclusion they reached in their 'roles' as first-century Christians.

For the following lesson we will continue the role-play, but this time each class member is the representative of a local *second*-century community, anxious to keep some link with the others. The task is to decide the best method of organization and to produce job specifications for each type of leader suggested.

When this has been completed I will introduce the students to Paul's letters and the Acts of the Apostles to see how close, or not, they have come to the practice of the early Church.

Second idea

It is important that at some time the pupils look at the way different Christian denominations approach the idea of authority and organization. The Christian experience over the centuries demonstrates that there is no obvious or easy way to determine what works best, or even what is inspired by God. The Orthodox and Catholic Churches tackled the problem from the top down, where organization begins with Christ and the apostles, who are seen as the founders of the Church. Their successors or descendants are the clergy, so they alone make the original Church present for today's Christians.

The Reformed tradition approached the problem from the bottom upwards. For them the entire Christian community are the Church, with everyone sharing in Christ's ministry. (In this sense base communities in the Roman Catholic Church are becoming part of the Reformed tradition.) We will explore how within the Reformed Churches there are differences, from the Quakers with no dependence on ministers, to the Presbyterian

Churches who place emphasis on the tradition of 'elders' and synods.

The Anglican tradition is especially interesting as being both Catholic and Reformed, thus uniting in itself a respect for both ways of government.

Third idea

This is not a new idea, but I have found it the most obvious and helpful way of introducing my pupils to the idea of priestly vocation. I show, at different times, three powerful television programmes which I have found inspiring and which capture all that is positive in the lives of good Christian men who have chosen to dedicate their lives to the service of others as ordained priests.

The first is a half-hour documentary on a day in the life of a delightful, smiling, Irish priest, Chris Conroy, who has chosen to live alone in a poor Andean village accompanying the people in their daily battle with poverty. He is not a revolutionary or a champion for new ways of celebrating liturgy or a leader of political rallies. He simply loves his people and shows them Christ's care and concern. I also invite into my class at this time my present parish priest, Father John, who also worked for some years in Peru. He and Father Chris have a lot in common. They are humanly warm and they laugh a lot.

The second documentary comes also from Latin America – the *Everyman* programme about El Salvador which features Jon Sobrino, the Jesuit priest whose community was murdered in his absence. He expresses, from the heart, everything that I have seen as positive in liberation theology. I have had many older students admit to me that the Church in El Salvador has given them a new understanding of Christianity that 'makes sense'.

The third programme is again about Christian witness in situations of human struggle. It is a documentary about a priest I have long admired, Archbishop Trevor Huddleston of the Anglican Church. The programme tells of his life and work for the abolition of the apartheid system in South Africa. My students have been deeply impressed by his integrity and his unwavering conviction that as a follower of Christ he had to become politically outspoken for the black population of South Africa, even when 'political Christianity' was frowned upon. The programme shows his extraordinary faith and courage in continuing to speak out against apartheid even after superiors recalled him to England during the troubles of the 1950s. 'Apartheid', he said, 'is not just a bad political system. Apartheid is a blasphemy.'

6

GOD IS LOVE

Jesus comes to his friends
when they love each other in their families,
as faithfully as Jesus did.

It was Blanca who pointed out to me the late-night television film that eventually proved to be a big hit in my RE lessons on marriage. Since *Make-Believe Marriage* was showing at midnight I presumed it was unsuitable viewing. But it turned out to be a charming and innocent film about a group of teenage American High School students whose teacher took a role-play method of approaching education in marriage and parenthood. He paired his students off, and over the course of a semester expected them to come up with solutions to the endless problems he threw at them. In the film, of course, the most unlikely couple finally grow to like each other and end up in a happy courting relationship 'for real'.

When I showed an extract from the film to my small class of the less academic 15-year-olds they begged me to pair them off too. With much laughter we took several lessons over our own version of the role-play game. The matching of partners was not easy, especially as two difficult and under-achieving boys were deliberately left out by the rest. I had to think quickly and invited them to be the officials we were going to need, registrar and cleric in the first instance.

The opening session gave me an excellent idea of these young people's attitudes towards marriage. The task was for each couple to plan, realistically, their future together. I had already given them their role: age, family background, occupation (or not). All seven couples eventually chose to get married, although two couples argued vehemently over this, the males wanting at first to cohabit. To begin with only four couples wanted church weddings, with three registry office ceremonies lined up; but as the discussions went on the positions shifted, and we ended up with seven church marriages. Two couples joined up for a double wedding, and with a sense of theatre invited all the rest to be bridesmaids, best men or fathers of the brides. We chose to 'celebrate' this particular event on the day our school chaplain took part by giving them a serious talk about the church marriage service and outlining it for them. We had a 'reception' of drinks and biscuits, plenty of music and, I hope, the memory of a happy RE class.

On the serious side the lessons taught me a great deal. When I came to gather information from the couples about the reasons for wanting a church wedding, only one couple mentioned the words 'God and blessing'. Unanimously they wanted a marvellous occasion; the girls all mentioned their dresses and the need to show them off to best advantage, and it was pointed out that the photos would look better taken outside a church! Three couples pointed out that they would have to marry in church or their parents would be too upset and might not even pay for a registry wedding. One girl said she would have to marry in church or her future babies wouldn't be accepted for christening. That struck up a good discussion: 'Why on earth do we want them christened?' asked her partner.

As I listened, like a fly on the wall, to many of the discussions and arguments between the pairs, one thing began to emerge strongly – as I would have expected. The pupils' ideas were almost always related strongly to their personal experience at home. Many of this group were disadvantaged, hence their under-achievement, and their attitudes accurately reflected the opinions or situations of their parents. The girl who wanted her children christened was one of the few from a nuclear family still attending church. Several of the couples presumed they would divorce quite quickly. I even heard one girl say (de-roling for the moment) 'I'm not having children. I don't want them to have a father like mine. I hate him.'

Nothing can be more difficult for the RE teacher today than this area of sexuality and the Christian ideal of marriage. The greatest sadness and pain is knowing that we have sitting in front of us young people with the widest variety of experiences possible of family life, and some of their experiences are tragic. Even though I teach in the privileged atmosphere of a Christian school, I know that what I want to share about the marvel and joy of sexual relationships, and the beauty of a committed marriage relationship that grows stronger over the years, will be totally 'unheard' by many of my pupils because of their own family experience. Why should they believe me when what they feel is hurt and disillusionment or grief over the loss of a parent, or bewilderment over the intensity of family rows? Because I teach in a Catholic school I have still more of a problem – the insistence of my Church authorities that I keep strictly to the unbending doctrines surrounding human sexuality, which in the last decades have become extraordinarily difficult to uphold in their entirety.

I have one advantage now, however, that I didn't have in my first years of teaching. I began my teaching career as a nun. That was a disadvantage for two reasons: first, I had no real credibility from the student's point of view; I remember my frustration when the young woman I was trying to influence on matters of sexual morality would cut me short with 'Well, what do you know about it, Sister?' But at a much more profound level it really was a disadvantage; the girls were right. Although I insisted to them (because I believed it myself) that I could understand the values of Christian marriage, I now realize that I didn't know the half of it! I became a nun because I was influenced by an exceptionally good RE teacher, who convinced me that I had to follow 'the better part' and become a wholehearted Christian. The world of sexuality, of material values and human ambition was presented as a great distraction to those wanting to follow the gospel. Extrovert and wholehearted in my response to everything – maybe because I am born a Gemini – I quite naturally took up the challenge. I had fourteen happy years of convent life and will be forever grateful for the experience. I learned about myself; I picked up the loving concern that these sisters had for disadvantaged young people, and it is a concern I have never been able to shed since. And I made life-time friends of generous, loving women, many of whom remain in the community and go on witnessing to Christ's preferences for the poor by their work with children deprived of ordinary needs. Perhaps I would still be part of their number had I not ended up teaching privileged middle-class girls in my old Finchley convent school (which was the one exception to their work for the poor). I asked to be transferred to a school which the sisters ran in a shanty town near Bogotá, but the days of foreign missionaries working abroad were over for my congregation. As Vatican II re-evaluated both the role of the nun and the role of the laity I began to grown uncertain of my vocation to religious life.

The decision to leave the convent was the most difficult choice I ever had to make. It is entirely against my nature – nothing virtuous about it – to give up a project unfinished or to renege on a promise. This was serious. I had promised to God that I would serve him for life under the vows of poverty, chastity and obedience. I also had my pride to deal with; how to tell my parents that I was going to change my mind? How to face a Catholic parish as a failed nun? But it didn't take me too long to reach my decision to apply for dispensation and start out on a new life at the age of thirty-five. I wanted to feel 'a person fully alive' so that the Glory of God could radiate through my life (as St Irenaeus suggested). But I was losing my ability to laugh and to enjoy every day as a gift. So when one morning I awoke in my Holloway convent and realized that I felt as imprisoned as my unhappy 'sisters' up the road my decision was made. In an instant I sat down and wrote for my dispensation, without a shadow of doubt about what I was doing. I had an extraordinary feeling of certainty about it.

I suspect that I am judged by the Christian community in a number of ways. Some nuns and priests will say that I made an original mistake and never had a real vocation to the religious life at all. Others will be more critical and accuse me of failing and turning my back on God for an easier way of life. The fact that I remain a 'practising' Catholic and that I teach RE will keep me in good standing with some people: 'Well, at least you are doing something worthwhile', one nun said to me! Others may well suspect that I am not fit to teach within the Church. Some lay Catholics are wary about ex-nuns; they have a respect for the 'higher calling' and therefore think of us as sinners who have failed to respond to the divine call we received. If divorce is frowned upon by these Christians, how much more the breaking of a vow to God. I understand their attitude but it is hurtful. In recent years I have become saddened by the knowledge that some parishioners talk about this behind my back whilst presenting friendly smiles to my face.

In some people's eyes my greater fault will have been to marry an ex-priest. A highly-skilled friend of mine was turned down for a job in a Catholic school (to teach French, as it happens) on the sole grounds that she was married to a former priest. She has never returned to teaching which is a great loss to the community and a great injustice to her. We were left in no doubt recently as to the suspicion we are held in, even by those we thought had accepted the situation. Bert was recommended to join the committee of a local ecumenical venture as he is well suited, by experience, to that particular role. The young Catholic priest present, however, vetoed the suggestion, saying, 'No, I can't recommend him; he has a dark secret.' That silenced the group of course, and set people's imagination astir. When later a friend pointed out to the chairperson of the group that the 'dark secret' was Bert's former position as a Catholic priest, the lady heaved a sigh of relief and said, 'Oh, is that all? I was imagining all kinds of scandal.' I can't pretend that actions like this don't hurt. All the more so because Bert and I have discovered in marriage a way to grow closer to God and more understanding of our fellow pilgrim travellers on the way.

Bert didn't leave the priesthood in order to get married, but marriage has proved for us a wonderful new vocation. His position as a Scripture lecturer in the Catholic Church became impossible when his bishop lost confidence in his work as principal of Corpus Christi College, London, a catechetical college which took on the reforms of Vatican II at a pace too fast for the hesitant authorities. Bert tried to remain within the system, but he was finally forced out by being denied any work either as a priest or a teacher. I have to say that we both look back now with no regrets about the past but with enormous relief that we have the joy of marriage and the privilege of parenthood. Nothing can be compared to the love parents feel when they see their children grow and take on (or take over) the skills and interests they had themselves. This week my two have been attending a holiday basketball school, and in their interest in the game I relive my own love for sport. I have got up early to get their kit washed and ironed afresh each day, remembering how proud I was at their age to look smart and prepared for every game. I see myself in my son as he reels off the names of every racing car driver in the Grand Prix, or recalls the name and achievement of any Olympic athlete or professional footballer at the drop of a hat. Bert feels the same as he listens to Blanca hum a tune in perfect pitch, or strum her guitar or recognize a piece of Beethoven or Vivaldi from hearing only a few bars of their music. We see ourselves in our children and we know instantly about resurrection!

I have been reflecting on this 'immortality' that parents enjoy through their children, because it is for me the most important part of the marriage, and by contrast the most vital sacrifice asked of the celibate. I had breakfast this Saturday morning listening to the BBC sports round-up. Alex Ferguson, manager of Manchester United, was talking of his boyhood in Aberdeen. He talked of his football-loving father, of whom he said, 'He gave me all the opportunities he never had, and somehow I am now what he was destined to be. I see my father in myself all the time.'

Through marriage a couple have this extraordinary possibility of living into the future; parenting is a participation in creation, even as it is a close communion with God. The Christian ideal of marriage has always presented parenthood as a profound mystery, in which God's love is mirrored in the love between man and woman that creates new life. So the Catholic Church's unwavering stand on marriage and birth issues is, in one sense, understandable to me. Part of me is proud to recognize that my Church refuses to present anything other than the highest ideal of family life.

At the same time, the publication of Pope John Paul II's encyclical *Veritatis Splendor* has filled me with anxiety. It has been praised for its courage in withstanding the creeping relativism of our age. But I am not sure that a creeping infallibilism is much of an answer. Certainly, its rigorous, restrictive tone won't endear it to my students.

When Pope Paul VI issued his encyclical *Humanae Vitae* in 1968, he stunned the Catholic world because people had genuinely expected a change in church discipline. Advisers had met in Rome for lengthy discussions on all aspects of marriage and birth control. An English delegate, Dr John Marshall, had gone to the Vatican convinced that church teaching couldn't change. He was amazed to find the discussion in his group so open and convincing that he altered his mind, so that in the end he, like the majority of others, recommended to the Pope a change in discipline over the use of contraceptives within marriage. Westminster's Cardinal Heenan remained more neutral, hedging his bets, although he publicly admitted that a change was not impossible. It is perhaps unfortunate that Cardinal Wotyjla, the future Pope John Paul II, never attended his group discussions to hear the frank opinions of others. He may just have been more open in those days to learn from others.

1993 is not 1968. No Catholics are expecting today, as people were then, that some change is going to be announced. We have come to recognize that our Polish Pope is strongly guided by the past. A strange title really, 'Veritatis Splendor', because it can be translated as 'the brightness of reality'. The problem for teachers is that 'reality' hits us in the face as we look across the desks and it is as far removed from papal exhortations as is the Popemobile from a Porsche.

Diarmaid MacCulloch, writing in *The Independent*, puts the

problem in perspective. Commenting on that word 'reality' in the document's title he says:

> But what is reality amid the sweaty delights of sex? The Vatican will repeat that reality is to be found in God's command to procreate the species. Good sex has the potential to produce children; bad sex is everything else. So bad sex includes heterosexual acts involving contraceptives; masturbation; gay sex of all sorts. On the propagation of this fatally simple idea among Roman Catholics, many of the world miseries now depend: the population explosion, the spread of Aids through unprotected sex, the victimisation of gay people.

The Roman Catholic Church's attitude towards sex has given the Church such a bad name amongst many of the young people I teach that it becomes almost impossible to offer positive guidance in sexual matters within the class-room context. I search for all that is positive about the beauty of human relationship in these documents (and *Humanae Vitae* offers me good material), but I do have a struggle to explain the prohibitions.

One way is to give my students a potted church history, explaining the background to the view adopted by the church authorities. I hope that the students don't throw the usual comments at me: 'But these rules are made by celibate males. They don't know anything about it.' I can't answer that one. I let history speak for itself. I explain that the Church's view was adopted, in the first place, from non-Christian sources. Early Christianity absorbed Greek culture and learning and so Greek philosophers, especially Aristotle, determined attitudes towards sex, rather than gospel teaching. Jesus had little to say about the details of human relationships and sexual activity. Aristotle wrongly presumed that the male carried the entire foetus in his semen; the woman was merely an incubator. This distortion from earliest days has contributed to every kind of wrong presumption. Clement of Alexandria took up this Greek idea and pronounced that 'to have sex for any purpose other than to produce children is to violate nature'. This Alexandrian idea had dominated Catholic teaching ever since, especially as Thomas Aquinas in the thirteenth century adopted it too. Other Christian denominations naturally modified this rigid teaching once the Reformed tradition allowed theologians and priests to marry. Thomas Cranmer, England's first married archbishop, when rewriting the marriage liturgy in 1549, specified that marriage existed not only for child bearing but 'for the mutual society, help and comfort that the one ought to have of the other'.

The use of contraceptives is not the only difficulty I have to deal with. Many of my classes will include children of divorced parents. I cannot possibly give a wholehearted exhortation on the indissolubility of marriage – even if I believed in it! And 'reality' is forcing me to reappraise my values on this issue too. I give, once again, an historical outline of the development of the sacrament of marriage as it evolved in the Roman Catholic tradition. It was St Augustine in the fifth century who said that marriage should be indissoluble, not only because Jesus had said this (Mark 10:6–10) but because it was a sign of the union between Christ and the Church. But I explain that for the next thousand years indissolubility was still seen as an ideal. Early bishops allowed divorce and remarriage, though for the husbands only (why do some people still maintain that the Church is not rooted in sexism?).

It was only in the thirteenth century that marriage was described as a sacrament, by Thomas Aquinas; and only in the sixteenth century that the Council of Trent introduced the strict law that made the indissolubility of the marriage partnership more than an ideal. I point out here that the Eastern Churches, perhaps because they never adopted the celibacy rule for all priests (hence remaining closer to the reality of people's sexual lives), have always allowed for divorce and remarriage, with the full blessing of the Church.

At this point in my lessons I discuss the ambiguous teaching about divorce in the Christian Churches, pointing to the confusion introduced very early on when Matthew seems to have modified Mark's words of Jesus: Mark's text (10:6–10) reads:

> God made them male and female and for this reason a man will leave his father and mother and unite with his wife, and the two will become one. So they are no longer two, but one. Man must not separate, then, what God has joined together . . . A man who divorces his wife and marries another woman commits adultery against his wife. In the same way, a woman who divorces her husband and marries another man commits adultery.(GNB)

Matthew adds an apparent exception to this rule: 'I say this to you: everyone who divorces his wife, except for the case of fornication, makes her an adulteress' (Matthew 5:31–32). In general, the Orthodox and Reformed Churches have followed the more liberal Matthew text, and allowed Christians to divorce when adultery has taken place. The Catholic Church applies the stricter ruling of Mark, and allows no divorce.

On the other hand, I also have to point out that the Catholic Church bends over backwards to free some people and enable them into a new marriage. The process of 'annulment' seeks to prove that the first marriage was invalid. In some cases this is clearly so, when for example the couple never actually had sexual intercourse. But it is difficult for some of us to see how a marriage that produced children, for example, can be called invalid on such grounds as 'immaturity at the time of the church wedding'. All of us are in a process of maturing, so where do we draw the line? I know several divorced couples who could probably seek and eventually obtain an annulment, but refuse the detailed and documented intrusion into the intimacy of the relationship that is required by the church enquiry.

The large number of restrictions and prohibitions mentioned in the preceding pages may give the impression that the only things that can be said about Christian marriage are negative ones. But then official Church teaching gives exactly that impression too. When a pope can travel half way across the world to Mexico, as he has done while I have been writing this chapter, and devote the whole of his first speech to the subject of contraception, one has to begin talking seriously in terms of obsession.

There is devastating flooding and famine in India, there is bloody fratricidal war in Somalia, there is unprecedented genocide in Bosnia, there is economic recession ruining the lives of countless people throughout Europe – and all the Vicar of Christ can talk about is what may or may not be done in bed. We wring our hands over today's teenage literature because it speaks of human relationships exclusively in terms of sex. But preoccupation with sexual morality is no less deplorable, since it has taught generations of Christians to identify the word 'sin' with sex, and in a world sick with greed, injustice, exploitation and oppression, to imagine that the only transgressions are sexual ones.

In a rapidly changing world, what is desperately needed at the moment is not a series of new prohibitions but a deeper understanding of where we stand and why. It is estimated that by the year 2000 four out of every five couples marrying for the first time in England and Wales will have cohabited first. This will be echoed in the United States and in Northern Europe. I can't ignore this when I prepare lessons on marriage for my pupils. Jack Dominian, the Catholic psychiatrist who has spent his life studying the institution of marriage within a faith context, points out that 'the complete sexual abstinence asked of previous generations is never likely to be re-established. All the psychological discoveries point the other way.' What is the cause for this? Sociologists give four reasons for the change.

First is the enormous increase in marital breakdown since the recent changes in the divorce laws. Young people don't want to repeat what happened to their parents and presume that 'trial marriages' will be the answer. (The facts now appearing in studies like John Haskey's *Population Trends* actually point to the reverse happening: couples who cohabit before marriage are in fact more likely to separate.)

A second reason for changed attitudes to marriage is the social fact that with careers available for women as well as men, most people now postpone their marriage to their late twenties. They do not however postpone their sexual activity. It is a biological fact that sexual energy is at its height in the late teens and early twenties. In earlier generations marriages took place at that time, but life expectancy was much shorter. A teenage bride today can anticipate a marriage lasting sixty or seventy years. Young people today may also argue that economic pressure is a good reason for sharing resources by living together.

The third reason is related: the emancipation of women once contraception was widely available, and women became free to enjoy 'leisure sex' for the first time. Women are becoming far more vocal in their rejection of the traditional church laws which in their eyes are an echo of machismo which devalues their femininity. The very church service itself colludes with the idea that the woman cannot speak for herself, but has to be handed over like a child by her father into the hands of her husband. Nowhere is this domination of men over women more apparent than in the Catholic tradition of Latin America. It is pungently expressed in Dorothee Soelle's writings. In one incident she describes her meeting with a group of women in a base community in the slums of Sao Paulo.

> When the word sexuality comes up, the otherwise very disciplined women suddenly begin to talk all at the same time. They tell of the lies they grew up with, of the ignorance about their own bodies, which they lived with for decades. 'The statue of the Virgin Mary in our bedroom was always draped with a towel when we slept together.'
>
> 'We were taught that we are dirty and only the Virgin is pure. In the country playing with boys was forbidden anyhow. In the end you are married and are supposed to sleep together with an animal that bites,' says a careworn old woman with flashing eyes. That she expresses this is a miracle, I think to myself.
>
> 'Sex is ugly' says another. 'Whoever dies a virgin is blessed because she is still innocent. That's the way I learned it.'
>
> 'It was nothing but torture for me whenever the man came again, but I didn't know how to defend or protect myself.'
>
> 'After the fourth child I simply couldn't any more, but I

couldn't get it across to him. Finally he disappeared, thank God.'

They all roared with laughter. On this afternoon I have understood that the theology of liberation cannot proceed from Rome but in fact issues from the poor. And the face of poverty is feminine. Without the conscious participation of women there is no liberation.

At the end I too say something about sexuality, namely that it is willed by God, a gift of creation, and above all a reason to praise God. This meets with tumultuous approval, and an old woman says: 'Say that again. Is that really in the Bible? We want to write it down and hang it up here.'[1]

The fourth reason for the change in the concept of marriage is the general decrease in religious practice in the Western world. Fewer and fewer people believe that a relationship can be effected, or altered, or improved by a certificate, or a marriage ceremony (especially a religious one), Against such odds, how are priests, Christian marriage advisers or teachers to convince young people that the sacrament of marriage is a life-giving relationship where the living God is to be found? One Catholic writer describes it beautifully:

> Christians not only enjoy what all married people who are striving to live a life of love enjoy, but out of their Christian heritage are able to name what is happening in their lives, share their understanding of it with their fellow Christians and celebrate it in their regular eucharists; and in this way are ready to offer those who do not accept their Christian beliefs something of the richness contained in the Christian story about marriage.[2]

I am with this author one hundred per cent. But how do I convey his vision to my teenagers?

When Bert and I were preparing to marry we were fortunate in having the encouragement and help of Bishop Butler, auxiliary bishop of the Westminster Diocese. When Cardinal Heenan died we discovered that he had never passed Bert's laicization papers on to Rome. Perhaps he was hoping Bert might change his mind. Bishop Butler speeded up the laicization process so that we could marry in our Catholic cathedral in Norwich on the day we had planned. I would have been deeply unhappy if my marriage was not blessed in the Catholic Church. With my deeply rooted Christian training a registry office wedding simply would not have done.

That I could marry in the setting of a nuptial Mass was the source of great joy therefore, for both our families and ourselves. But it raised immediate question marks in my mind about the logic of the church system. Why were we being allowed a second start with the Church's blessing, while divorced Catholics remain barred from remarriage in the prayerful setting of a church service?

Pope Paul VI was quite ready to offer laicization to those priests who asked for it in the years immediately following the upheaval of the Vatican Council. Was he being illogical in refusing the same facilities to those whose marriage had broken down?

Is Pope John Paul II being rather more logical in the hard-line attitude he takes towards both married people and priests? Very few priests who have asked him for laicization have been granted it. Former priests who wish to marry are treated like divorced Catholics. This means that they are alienated from the Church at the very time when they most need the comfort of their Christian community.

Last year I was deeply shocked to discover the closing of ranks amongst the clergy over this issue. We had invited Bruce Kent to speak to our sixth-formers on United Nations' issues, within a programme of liberal studies which is part of every sixth-form syllabus. Probably none of the students present knew anything of his former life as a priest, certainly no one knew whether he was married or not. His talk and skill as a leader of debate were greatly appreciated by our students and we, the RE staff, were impressed by the 'Catholic' input he gave, reporting and praising successive popes or church councils for promoting human rights and social justice in a number of important areas. A few days later we received a letter from the bishop and the local deanery of priests – signed by all but one priest – severely reprimanding us for inviting into the school a man who was 'not in good standing with the Church'. His only mistake it seems to me, is not that he was forced to marry without the Church's blessing, but that he sought laicization from priesthood in the pontificate of the wrong pope. Bert was able to marry me because he sent in his application a little earlier.

This obsession with law and discipline upsets me. It is far removed from the Jesus of the gospels who regularly put aside the requirements of religious law when it contradicted the requirements of love. This gospel is simply no longer recognizable in the inflexible Church law on marriage issues. How can someone who has given his whole life to the service of truth, justice and peace – in a world gone mad with war, injustice and hatred – be deprived of the Christian blessing of his marriage to a wife who works untiringly for the same causes, inspired by the same gospel values? Bruce Kent is, I know, deeply hurt by the rejection of the Church he has served and loved so faithfully as a prophetic voice for peace. He works now in the State schools. They give him an enormous welcome.

What should be the Church's role vis-à-vis human relationships? My own profoundly happy experience has not blinded me to the struggle and deep unhappiness of many people. I would be foolish to write in glowing terms of the wonderful grace given by the sacrament of marriage, enabling couples to live blissfully as images of God's faithful love. Human beings and the human situation are flawed from the start, so married life is like an obstacle race. I see the Church's role as being that of an encouraging bystander who picks up the bruised competitors after every stumble, binding their wounds and urging them on towards the finishing line. Unfortunately what the Church actually does is to set up many of the hurdles and then disqualify couples or individuals for the slightest hesitation or fall.

This came home to me powerfully when I met the mother of one of my students in the supermarket. She engaged me in the aisle for twenty minutes, relieved, she said, to find someone with whom she could share her worries. Her daughter had apparently talked to her about an RE lesson when I had listened to the idealistic and 'unorthodox' views of the class concerning relationships. 'You don't seem like the RE teachers we had at school, who told us what we could or couldn't do without ever listening to us,' she said. I discovered, in those twenty minutes, an integrity and compassion in this woman who worked in the family clinic, carrying the pain and hurt of countless children and their parents. It taught me a great deal. Listening and not imposing authoritative obligations on people was her way of enabling them to cope with life. 'If only', she said, 'I had the support of my Church. Instead, I only too often come up against the guilt and hurt caused by unbending Church legislation. I don't know how to respond to this, though I remain a Catholic myself.'

Time and again the Catholic marriage difficulties of my friends take me by surprise. One couple asked my advice when their twins were reaching the age for first communion. I discovered that these regular church-goers and devoted Christian parents carried the pain of a non-recognized marriage which barred the Catholic partner (the mother) from receiving communion. This was her first marriage and the only sexual relationship she had ever had, but her husband had married before, briefly, whilst at university. He had married his university girlfriend in the Anglican church because he valued Christian marriage and refused to have pre-marital sex, unlike his student friends. But at nineteen they were very young and hardly knew each other; eighteen months later they parted. Sally, my friend, had presumed his divorce would not affect her, and so prepared for her Catholic wedding, only to discover it was denied her because of his divorce. She suffered agonies over the loss of a church wedding and the subsequent bar from receiving the Eucharist. Her pain was resurrected as her children prepared for the sacrament. I advised her to speak with her parish priest whom I recognized as a caring and sympathetic man. He assured her that it could be 'fixed up' in time, and that she would be able to receive communion alongside her daughters. But as the day approached he told her that there was nothing he could do, and that he must continue to refuse her communion because 'some people here may know of your illicit position'. Sally wept at her children's first communion celebration. Her Anglican husband, a faithful Mass-attender alongside his family, wished he had opted for pre-marital sex with his first companion, instead of marriage!

Is it really any wonder if many Catholics lose faith in their Church's credibility over sexual marriage issues? I try hard in class to avoid sharing the cynicism that I feel. To do this I point to the examples I know of contented, fulfilling marriage relationships that do seem strengthened and illuminated by Christian faith. A young Catholic couple, close friends of ours, agreed to contribute to a school textbook on Christianity that I was asked to write. I'm glad to record that the reaction of my pupils to John and Mary's honest revelation about their relationship is one of quiet admiration, and I detect a sense of relief in the more protected students, those who are set positive, Christian ideals by loving and secure parents whose sacramental marriage has worked well. I am learning that there are young people for whom the sexual permissiveness of this age is actually a great anxiety and burden. John and Mary wrote:

> The ban on pre-marital sex was something we committed ourselves to over six years of courtship. It wasn't easy, especially as we were seen to be swimming against the tide. But having to verbalise our feelings for each other instead of simply expressing them physically taught us a respect for each other and a skill in communication which has remained. The experience has given us now a secure and trusting marriage, where there is no fear of letting each other down.

That paragraph pays a moving tribute to the self-sacrifice of which generous youngsters are capable. There are students in my class who find strength and encouragement in such an example. But there are many who would want to underline that such selflessness has to be a gift made by the couple, not simply an act of obedience to authority. When ideals are expressed only in negatives, in prohibitions, and in absolutes, they can be counter-productive for many of today's youth.

Even Catholic writers like Dr Jack Dominian confirm this. He has always stressed the truth that it is the couple who make the commitment to one another, not the Church. He points out that most scholars agree that the biblical Song of Songs is a celebration of the physical union between a betrothed couple. He goes as far as saying that whilst it would be impossible to approve promiscuous, adulterous or prostituted sex, it becomes very difficult to condemn categorically, as intrinsically wrong, pre-marital sexual intercourse as one part of an exclusive and faithful, growing relationship leading into marriage. He is saying that the Church needs to see marriage as a process which develops over a lifetime of love and determination. The couple, who, after all, give one another the sacramental foundation of the union, should be left responsible for their sexual behaviour. My students would not have too much difficulty with this view.

Some resolutions for the class-room

First idea

The role play I described at the beginning of this chapter needs some development. Each week I could introduce to my 'couples' the different hurdles that people have to face in their relationships and in family life. The whole area of parenthood and family needs investigation. My couples could be presented with a variety of situations:

- You want to start a family but discover that it is not possible for you. How will you cope with childlessness?
- Your birth-control programme goes awry and you find a child is expected. How will you respond to an unplanned pregnancy?
- Your first baby is born handicapped. How will you react?
- Your family has a history of life-threatening disease passed on through the male. Would you consider artificial insemination by donor to prevent the problem in your family?
- The male partner is made redundant and can't find work.

What solution will you seek, in view of your young family?

- Your elderly mother becomes dependent when your father dies. She wants to live with you. Your husband/wife is unhappy with the situation. What will you do?
- Your 17-year-old son announces he is gay. What is your reaction?

The class need to discuss these and other issues in some detail, so that they are free to offer their own opinions and values. Then it would be most helpful to introduce to them adults who have had to face similar situations. There is nothing like true-life experience.

I have many worthwhile discussions with my classes, when appropriate, on adoption as a means of parenthood because this is my own experience. The most successful classes are always when a teacher can say 'I feel this deeply and I'm willing to share it with you.' My experience of miscarriages, the dark pain of feeling a failure as a woman, and the struggle to adopt because of restrictive laws in our country – this has given me an authenticity before my students that nothing else could replace. I tell them that I have no time for the over-religious view that was offered me by a fellow Christian trying to sympathize over my inability to conceive children: 'It is obviously God's will that you are infertile because by adopting children from the poverty of South America you and Bert have made your marriage worthwhile.' What a strange view, as though God could step in and intervene and put my hormonal disorder back in working order if he really wanted to. I am forced, over and over again in religious education lessons (whatever the topic), to return to the fundamental question 'What kind of God do you believe in?'

Second idea

I have to admit to some hesitation in inviting visitors to my classes from over-enthusiastic religious groups. I am disappointed that the Life Movement has fallen into this category. We used to invite speakers to introduce the pupils to the work of Life members in upholding the value of the life of an unborn child, and in assisting women or girls through pregnancy as an alternative to abortion. However, the films and literature this organization has produced, with its deliberate and emotional shock, tends to be counter-productive. I find some pupils become quite outlandish in their reaction to the dogmatic approach taken by the speakers. Young people want to be presented with views in a more neutral way, with no emotional blackmail, for that only guarantees their opposition. I am lucky to have found a Catholic doctor who speaks quite openly on fertility, abortion, contraception and all the related issues of medical ethics. He doesn't try to force a 'Catholic' view on to the students and yet, by his integrity and honesty, he inspires them to think very deeply about the highest ideals associated with family life. Long may this good doctor live near me.

Third idea

God bless the makers of soap operas! The most powerful aid I have in the class-room these days is the television set and the video machine. If you can't beat them, so they say, you must join them. 98 per cent of my pupils seem to watch all the soap operas. I may not approve of so much television but it is a fact I cannot alter. I am not innocent myself, as I watch the early evening Australian variety with the children and the slightly later very English *Coronation Street* and *Eastenders* with my husband. My excuse to dismissive friends and colleagues is that I need the information for school.

And this is not idle talk. Many of the young people in my classes have suffered or are suffering from a variety of experiences portrayed on the screen. Our class situation may be their only opportunity to express or explore their feelings about home situations. I can offer them the safety of disguise behind the television character or story-line. This year one girl entered deeply into a discussion about the disruption of family life brought about by a teenage pregnancy, when we had taken as our discussion point the unexpected pregnancy of a *Home and Away* character. I only learnt, later, when she lingered behind to tell me, that her 17-year-old sister had been pushed into an abortion by family pressure. It was obviously an unresolved worry for them all.

At parents' evening I always encourage parents – who frequently sigh over the television habits of their children – to sit down and watch the programme with them. I am surprised that this has never occurred to some parents. Blanca, Pedro and I have had some wonderful talks about sexuality and responsibility and the values and beauty of relationships, where respect for one another is the foundation. Like every parent I worry about my children and have no idea whether my way of parenting is the right one. But television-sharing is one important way of giving time to the family and listening to their views.

7

YOU DID IT UNTO ME

> Jesus comes to his friends
> when they are close to dying
> and their friends comfort them.

My mother died without receiving the last, comforting sacrament of our Church, the 'anointing of the sick'. The news of her sudden death, which was broken to me at the hospital, had the strange effect of filling me with a sense of loss on her behalf. My immediate reaction was to ask the nurse to send for the priest to give my mother this prayerful reassurance that she was in God's hands. Of course it could make not the slightest difference to her at this point, but I needed her to have this final blessing. To my great surprise and comfort the nurse told me that they had sent for the priest already. In the event the hospital chaplain was never traced as it was his day off. But the policeman, who was at the hospital to assist at the identification process, was quickly on his radio sending police officers to local churches to find a substitute. Several hours later, when I had left the hospital to be with my father, we had a phone call to tell us that a priest and a Catholic nurse had said prayers at my mother's side. I felt much better.

As the shock of my mother's death eased I realized that the greatest help I had experienced was from the sensitive care I had received from the nurse, the young police officer and a neighbour at the hospital. There was gentleness, respect, a warm cup of tea, the offer to find anyone I needed and to phone all the family, and a comforting arm around my shoulders. At this saddest moment of my life, in a strange hospital, God was certainly not absent for I was upheld by human prayer, and by compassion and understanding. 'Where is love and loving kindness, God is fain to dwell.'

Sickness, dying and death make us vulnerable, brittle beings. As I have grown older I have come to appreciate that Christian discipleship consists fundamentally in embracing Jesus' work of healing, for healing was an intrinsic part of his ministry. Jesus was uncompromising in his hostility to all forms of sickness, bodily, mental or spiritual, because he saw it as a burden that deprived people of the wholeness that is their birthright as sons and daughters of God, born in his image. It is clear that the Church from the earliest times saw itself as a healing Church simply because it is the Church of Jesus Christ, commissioned to continue his ministry. As Mark reported it: 'These are the signs that will be associated with believers . . . they will lay their hands on the sick, who will recover' (Mark 16:17–18, JB). The Catholic sacrament of anointing the sick rests firmly on the practice of the early Christians recorded by St James:

> If one of you is ill, he should send for the elders of the Church, and they must anoint him with oil in the name of the Lord and pray over him. The prayer of faith will save the sick man and the Lord will raise him up again; and if he has committed any sins, he will be forgiven. (James 5:14–15, JB)

Some Christians take this text to suggest that with enough prayer and faith individuals can get up from 'terminally ill' sick-beds, miraculously cured. I have Christian friends who meet daily in prayer, convinced that their petitions can persuade God to intervene and cure the sick when all medical help has failed. I admire their faith in a way, but I can't say I share it. And I don't feel deprived. The help they seek for people is too particular for me and suggests that God could, if he so wished, remove all the pain and suffering that exists in the world. The sight of the little Bosnian girl on our television screens as I write this, with her broken and shrapnelled body, is enough evidence for me that God doesn't sit back and wait to be asked for his help. He would be a monster if he could take away her pain and doesn't do so.

I can understand that whenever we come face to face with suffering our instinct is to ask God for help and if the suffering continues, at best we blame God for it, at worst we lose faith in him altogether. I really find this a problem when I start to analyse it. Whenever I ask my pupils about prayer and what that word means to them, they invariably come up with answers like 'Asking God to help the people in Bosnia'. Petitionary prayer is what many people mean by prayer. I admit it is one aspect of prayer, but it is the most difficult one to get right. My memories are of primary-school nun-teachers telling me that God will always answer my prayers, even if sometimes he gives a definite 'no' as an answer. I used to think, 'What a cop out; you can't actually argue with that one.' But this reasoning still comes from pulpits and, as I know only too well from my agnostic pupils, is destined to relegate all prayer for some of them to the bin labelled 'Not for me, thank you'.

If I don't believe that God will save the life of the Bosnian child if only enough of us ask for help in prayer, does it mean I no longer believe in prayer? Not at all. I do believe in prayer and I do pray – rather a lot actually. But the purpose of prayer isn't to change God. It is, quite simply, to change ourselves. If all the Catholic families in Croatia, and all the Orthodox families in Serbia, were praying and begging God for peace in their land, and in the silence of their prayer felt the presence of God who is love and compassion and forgiveness, surely they would find a way to stop the hatred. They would answer their own prayers by recognizing God in the heart of the sorrow they were causing one another. Prayer may indeed be the only way to heal a very sick world.

The sacrament of the sick has always been the least attractive of all the sacraments, for it evolved into the final rite performed by the priest when all hope was lost and a patient had no chance of recovery. So it was associated with anxiety and loss. But this has changed in recent years and the sacrament, by a dramatic change of emphasis, now celebrates what I see as the very heart of the gospel – a loving community that is able to comfort and draw a sick person out of a sense of isolation. In other words, it celebrates in the name of the Church the kind of healing that I experienced at the hospital by the human understanding of those who 'ministered' to me at my mother's death. I find once again that a sacrament of the Church is simply and powerfully a celebration in religious terms of ordinary, human actions that occur whenever love is present. For where love is there is God.

The experience of sickness is a profound intrusion into life. Peter Wilkinson expresses clearly the sense of alienation that it can bring.

> Sickness is a moment filled not only with physical pain and suffering but also with a sense of alienation and isolation, fear and uncertainty. One aspect of this alienation is that a sick person becomes acutely aware of his own body – its pain, its numbness, its nausea. Alienation and isolation are further experienced at the level of being withdrawn from normal everyday life. This means being confined to bed, either at home or in hospital, isolated from all those activities which make life worth living.
>
> Sickness involves a marginal existence which seems only to speak of exclusion from the life that matters. The world of the sick person shrinks to the size of the bedroom and challenges all the basic assumptions we take so much for granted. In such circumstances, a sick person feels that he or she has nothing to contribute except to remain in a state of total helplessness. And the sense of alienation is completed by the feeling of abandonment by God himself.[1]

As my mother grew older she suffered physically, often acutely, from arthritic hips. She had a first hip-replacement operation in the local hospital, and although she hated the thought of hospitalization, the experience brought enormous relief from pain. She had nothing but praise for those who cared for her. When she returned to hospital a year later for the second hip replacement we all expected a wonderful recovery and her happy return to pain-free walking. But it didn't turn out that way. The hip operation went well and her pain ceased. But in its place she experienced utter misery. The source of her new suffering was the change of economic policy in the hospital, which resulted in a reduced number of nursing staff and made it necessary to put meals out to tender. This meant that patients rarely saw a nurse, and received cold, unimaginative meals. According to a rather vocal lady in the small ward, these were 'thrown at us at the very end of their run, and by this time the meals were completely cold and inedible, and the staff wanted to get home'.

My non-complaining mother, who always feared being a nuisance to anyone, suffered acute anxiety about the intestinal problem that arose out of not eating properly. Her irritable bowel syndrome returned which meant she needed the toilet at a moment's notice, but there was rarely a nurse to respond to her bell. So she would get herself to the toilet and sit there until a nurse would return her to her bed, scolding her like a child for breaking the rules. They even found her one night asleep on the toilet. She admitted to me later that she felt humiliated, scared and a burden to the nurses. I wept inside that none of us, her family, had been able to give her the comfort in sickness that she had always given us. In a way, the success of the expensive NHS hip-replacement operation had been negated by the money-saving changes that the hospital made, which denied patients the actual care they need – human contact with people and meals lovingly cooked and served.

I can see here a most wonderful opportunity for Christian groups who want to find an authentic way to follow the gospel. I could envisage a religious order, for example, of men or women or both who would work in our NHS hospitals around the clock. What a difference it would make to the sick in hospital wards if the cooks, the cleaners, the nurses and doctors were assisted by people motivated by the gospel concern to ease the mental and spiritual hurt that accompanies the physical suffering. Hospital chaplains need a community of helpers around them, to listen and love and so partake in the healing process themselves. I can almost envisage a resurrection of religious life. This would not be an adaptation of any of the existing religious orders, which were founded to counteract the dehumanizing poverty-stricken conditions of another world. The money-orientated world of today is an expression of a different sort of inhumanity and poverty. Could there be a host of generous souls waiting in the wings, only asking to be organized to deal with it?

Cost-efficiency has produced a sick world, where people's simple needs are no longer considered, not even at the time they most need sensitive and delicate consideration. To take a simple example. A six-week-old baby had died. She was buried holding the teddy bear given her by her grieving sisters. The heartbroken parents planned a headstone decorated with a small bear. The church authorities in charge of the cemetery refused permission, explaining that rabbits were within the new regulations but not bears. Could a TV script-writer have invented anything more ludicrous?

My own family was faced with similar farcical restrictions at the cemetery where we buried my mother. In the name of economy, care of the cemetery has been cut down to a minimum, leaving us with only two kinds of headstone to choose from, and forbidding us to put flowers on the grave. How people actually feel about such penny-pinching is never asked, even when it causes them deep distress. Imagine my horror on a recent visit to discover that the reduced force of council workers had put my mother's headstone on someone else's grave. In fact it took three attempts to put several misplaced stones in the right place. When I spoke to one elderly man whose wife's grave was adorned with someone else's stone, he wept as he said, 'I was rooted to the spot when I walked into the cemetery. I felt they had taken Evelyn away. I am devastated that they couldn't even get this right.'

I fear for the future of our Western society where human needs are being increasingly sacrificed in the name of 'efficient management'. In contrast the poverty of Third-World countries results in an increase in human tenderness and sensitivity. I realize now that there is something positive in the destitution of an African hospital, where relatives bring food for their loved ones and sit patiently for hours, waving the flies away from their wounds. There is a moving ambiguity about the tragedy of death in Latin American homes. It is such a frequent visitor that families lovingly attend their graves sitting on the ground talking, singing, picnicking alongside their deceased parents or children. I often tell my classes these days that we are the poor, not those in developing countries who struggle to find food. They look at me a bit surprised, but I think most understand what I mean.

There is a very fine video produced by Tear Fund called *Women Like Us* which makes this point very well. It shows the strength and determination of impoverished women in South America who work in terrible conditions, for long hours, and for pitiful pay. Against all the odds they find ways to provide for their children. By contrast the frivolous comments made by the Western women in the film ('Of course they are poor, they don't work as hard as us'; 'Well, they have so many children I don't suppose they mind too much when some die'; 'It is their own fault that they are poor. People like that don't know how to help themselves') are so superficial that my students immediately recognize a different kind of poverty. They also ask me, on viewing films like this one, the age-old questions: 'What is suffering?' 'How can God let people suffer like this?' 'Does God suffer too?' In other words, we come back again to the most basic of all religious questions, 'What kind of God do you believe in?'

As I come towards the end of my reflections on pilgrimage I realize that the God I believe in is the God of the poor; the God who can speak to those who suffer because he suffers with them. For this reason I put a high priority on this sacrament of the sick and remind my class of Pope John Paul II's words when he attended a public celebration of anointing the sick at St George's Cathedral, Southwark, in 1982: 'Do not neglect your sick and elderly. Do not turn away from the handicapped and the dying. Do not push them to the margins of society. For if you do, you will fail to understand that they represent an important truth . . . that weakness is a creative part of human living.' If weakness is a creative part of living, can it be said that God, the creator, knows weakness and vulnerability? I find this such an absorbing question that I have spent much time with our sixth-form students exploring it.

Is it possible for God to suffer? My immediate, spontaneous answer is 'yes'. The more I think about it, the more certain I am that the God I believe in agonizes over the world he created.

Now, how is it that I can feel so sure that God is vulnerable when, as a Roman Catholic Christian, I belong to a tradition which for centuries has held the opposite view? My agnostic or atheistic friends may say, of course, that I don't know what I'm talking about anyway. They echo in their own way the words of the eighth-century desert mystic John of Damascus: 'The only thing we know about God is that he cannot be known.' But his conclusion did not stop him believing, or exploring.

I am part of a Christian community that has inherited centuries of philosophical and theological ideas about God. One thing seems quite clear. There has never been one, simple, description of God which is definitive. Each age has produced thinkers, who, influenced by their own times, have made attempts to describe the God who 'cannot be known'.

I have asked ten Christians the question 'Is it possible for God to suffer?', telling them to answer quickly with a spontaneous reply. Seven answers, laced with 'ums' and 'oh dears', were fairly definite that God could not possibly suffer because if he did he would not be God. These answers are heavily dependent upon a picture of God formed by the abstract philosophical thinking of the early Greek 'Fathers of the Church'. This thinking was eventually inherited by Thomas Aquinas, the thirteenth-century philosopher.

As Roman Catholics my seven friends were undoubtedly influenced by Aquinas. Until recently his teachings occupied a unique position in the Church as the basis of theological and philosophical studies in Roman Catholic seminaries. (Hence they still influence most Sunday sermons.) Aquinas, in his most famous work *Summa Theologiae* speaks of the attributes of God: existence, life, power, wisdom and will. These features are known to us through our own experience of them. We exist. We live. We know what it is to be powerful or wise. The question for philosophers was whether these features could also be attributed to God in an absolute way. Aquinas gave his opinion in answer to the Jewish philosopher, Moses Maimonides, who had died just twenty years before Aquinas was born. Maimonides had postulated that it was only possible to attribute one feature to God – that God is One.

Aquinas was able, by using what was called analogous language, to add other attributes to God. God, he said, is not only One, he is Personal, Holy, Omnipresent, Omnipotent, Omniscient, Immortal, Good and Immutable. It seems to me that the reluctance of my seven friends to accept a suffering God is based on this picture of God. For these attributes, especially when raised to infinity, make God into an impassive, immovable, cold, distant reality, unaffected by our own small, unimportant lives.

Suffering for us is caused by physical pain, by loss, by broken relationships or by unattainable desires. These causes of suffering are all imperfections which can be measured against their opposites: the pain of a young woman dying of cancer against the exuberant energy of a fit young athlete winning the 100 metres final; or the misery of the redundant worker measured against the fulfilled joy of the newly promoted head of department. Suffering is associated with failure, with limitations, with powerlessness, with ignorance and with all less than perfect situations. According to the philosophical attributes of God, he lies outside these imperfections. God cannot fail, he has no limits, he is all-powerful, he is all-knowing, he can't change as he eternally IS. Such a God cannot suffer because he is perfect and suffering lies in the absence of perfection.

God must be thought to have whatever quality it is better to have than not to have. That is to say, God cannot have qualities which it is preferable to be without. But since it is assumed to be better to be without suffering than to suffer, God must be incapable of suffering. On these grounds God is considered to be necessarily 'impassible', unsuffering.

Three of my ten friends disagreed with this verdict of the seven. One of them put it this way: 'Can God suffer? Isn't our

Christian God the same as the God of the Jewish people? Didn't he walk alongside his people? I suspect he does suffer then. Can you imagine a father not suffering if his children get into trouble, or lose their way or suffer disaster? Parents suffer more for their children than the children suffer themselves.'

I can remember to this day the anguish I felt when my daughter severely fractured her elbow. The sight of her silent tears when the calpol effect wore off and her aching arm, hanging in traction, nagged her with persistent pain, made me feel so helpless that I hardly knew what to do for her or for myself! The heart of the world goes out to the father of the young Bosnian girl I mentioned earlier, for the agony on his face as he sat by Irma's bedside is unforgettable.

This is a very different view of God. Of course many of the attributes discovered by Aquinas are also mentioned in the Hebrew Bible. But the biblical understanding of God is very different from the medieval philosophical one. The biblical attributes are never abstract.

One of God's attributes is his immutability. In philosophical language, this means that he is not changeable. This implies that God is static, invulnerable, unaffected by anything that ever happens outside himself. His immutability leaves him immune to suffering, as we have seen. The Hebrew Bible also says that God is immutable – yet in quite a different sense. The Hebrew word used is *emeth*. It means that God is unchangeable in his trustworthiness, in his reliability; he is the rock on which we stand.

> In times of trouble he will shelter me;
> he will keep me safe in his Temple
> and make me secure on a high rock.
> (Psalm 27:5, GNB)

But God is not unchangeable full stop. He has other attributes too, and obviously each attribute must be qualified by the others. So *emeth* is qualified by God's *hesed*. *Hesed* is, for the Jew, God's most distinctive characteristic. *Hesed* means loving compassion.

God stands firm, unmoved, never wavering *in his parental compassion for his children.* Now such a God, suggests my friend number eight, must suffer alongside his family. I agree with her. By loving compassion we empathize with others; we suffer with them and this makes us as vulnerable as they are in their pain.

There is a delightful story in the Bible of Abraham entering into a typical Eastern bargaining agreement with God (Genesis 18:16ff). God seems set on destroying the sinful Sodom. Abraham is concerned that the innocent will be destroyed alongside the guilty. God says he will spare the city if fifty innocent people can be found. Abraham starts the bargaining and gets God to change his mind several times while he knocks the number down to ten. The story presumes a God who is vulnerable, able to be influenced by his people's cries for help. He is a God of the soft heart. From our human experience we know that 'soft hearts' are most likely to be found in those who know suffering.

My ninth friend was unhesitating in her reply to my question 'Can God suffer?' 'Well, of course he can,' she said. 'Jesus is God and Jesus died on the cross. Therefore God died on the cross. You can't die on a cross without suffering.' I found her language very clumsy but I can sympathize with what she is saying.

I don't say any more, as I used to, that Jesus is God without any further qualification. I have reverted to the biblical way of speaking, where the word God is reserved for the Mystery whom Jesus called 'Father'. Of that mystery Jesus can be called the Son, or Mirror, or Servant, or Word, or Expression, but he never claimed identity. Jesus is not the object of our searching or journeying: he points us to the Father (he is my signpost).

My friend was speaking in trinitarian language, a legacy of fifth-century and medieval philosophical speculation. Any language we try to use to speak of God is necessarily difficult, and the language problem may well be responsible for the many heresies which developed in the early centuries when Christians struggled with Christology – the attempt to demonstrate the precise relationship between God and Jesus. If my friend meant by saying 'Jesus is God' that Jesus is not human as we are, then she is really a Monophysite and she was condemned at the Council of Chalcedon in AD 451!

But I do agree with my ninth friend that when Jesus, innocent of any crime, died as a criminal on an execution tree, God could not have remained uninvolved. According to medieval theology, Jesus had to die because God demanded justice in 'satisfaction' for human sin. And Anselm (1033–1109) had suggested a theory of 'atonement' for sin. God had been injured by sin and man had caused the injury. Only a 'God-man' could bring together the two parties for reconciliation. Thus Anselm introduced the phrase 'God became man' in Jesus. It is an easy step from this theology to say, as my friend says, 'Jesus is God'. I don't find this salvation imagery very helpful. It reduces God to an unfeeling judge who demands his pound of flesh. When I look at the cross it is through the eyes of the Gospel writers who never use such *legalistic* language to discuss the meaning of Jesus' death. The New Testament writers turned more easily to the language of *revelation*, as I mentioned in my reflections on the Eucharist in chapter 2. They believed that Jesus' death revealed God. They believed that Jesus, in his life and death, revealed a new understanding of God. He embodied Godliness in a truly human life. Where the human temptation is to think of God as distant and judgemental, Jesus portrayed God as being close, compassionate, forgiving, merciful and understanding.

Jesus is a window into God. Look at Jesus and you can know God. To see Jesus is to see God. And nowhere was this more evident than in his accepting even death on a cross, without hitting back. God didn't demand Jesus' death. Sinful people demanded it. God forgives even the murderers of his son.

Jesus would have been surprised to find that his understanding of God was seen as 'new'. He based his teachings on his own meditation on the Hebrew Bible. It was there that he found evidence enough of a compassionate, merciful God who walked alongside his people. He would have understood this, for example, from the prophet Hosea who gives a wonderful description of God as a Father who cannot bring himself to punish Israel, his wayward child. It is a picture of a Father who suffers agony over the wilfulness of an adolescent who has to learn the hard way.

> The Lord says,
> 'When Israel was a child, I loved him
> and called him out of Egypt as my son.
> But the more I called him,
> the more he turned away from me.
> My people sacrificed to Baal;
> they burned incense to idols.
> Yet I was the one who taught Israel to walk.
> I took my people up in my arms,
> but they did not acknowledge that I took care of them.
> I drew them to me with affection and love.
> I picked them up and held them to my cheek;
> I bent to them and fed them . . .
> "How can I give you up Israel?
> How can I abandon you? . . .
> My heart will not let me do it!
> My love for you is too strong." '
>
> (Hosea 11:1–8, GNB)

The Gospel writers tell us that this same compassionate and vulnerable, parent-like God is revealed to them most fully in Jesus' own life. And most especially in his death. Christian people who work with the dying have expressed something of this certainty about God's loving presence sustaining those who suffer the agony of dying or those who suffer their loss.

These people don't need theological or philosophical arguments to argue the case whether God suffers or not. They experience a faith certainty that God weeps with them because he knows what suffering is. I find this most movingly expressed in *Good Friday People* by Sheila Cassidy. She invites us to share the pain of people who (she believes) share deeply in Jesus' own story of suffering. Their journeys go beyond the cross and in some mysterious way are united to the suffering of God himself. She says the book is about 'sharing as far as we are able in the suffering of the world, which is also the suffering of God'. Sheila Cassidy, herself once tortured in a Chilean prison, tries to give a meaning to suffering by describing the terrible ordeal of Elie Wiesel in Auschwitz. He describes the execution of a small boy in the camp.

> For more than half an hour he stayed there, struggling between life and death, dying in slow agony under our eyes. And we had to look at him full in the face. His tongue was still red, his eyes were not yet glazed. Behind me I heard the same man asking: 'Where is God now?' And I heard a voice within me answer him: Where is he? Here he is – he is hanging here on this gallows.

Sheila Cassidy concludes:

> Is that what gives meaning to suffering? Is it because God is in it, in it with us, that the obscene becomes transformed into the holy? I don't know but I believe it is. God is hanged in Auschwitz, he is raped and shot in El Salvador, he dies of AIDS in a London flat.[2]

The last of the ten friends whom I questioned knows the God of the process theologians. He would feel great sympathy with Sheila Cassidy. His reply to my question was, 'Yes, of course God suffers. I see God as the Ground of my Being. I have suffered and God was present.' I should say that this friend has been studying a panentheistic view of God by reading theologians like Teilhard de Chardin, Tillich, Whitehead, Hartshorne and Norman Pittenger.

The theory these philosophers have developed is known as process theology. It is based on the truism that anything which stops changing is dead. To live is to change. We speak of a living God (or else he is nothing), hence God must change. If everything we experience is change, activity, moving forward, it must be grounded on a Reality of this same kind. Their panentheistic theology speaks of everything being in God, so that all that occurs is immediately experienced by God who is affected by it, and responds to it.

This, of course, requires a new way of interpreting the philosophical attributes of God, which in philosophical analysis seem so static and cold. God is not 'outside time' (eternal) but time-bound – for the future is of course undetermined if God is affected by on-moving experiences.

He is unknowing of the undetermined future. And God is not impassive and immutable, for he is changed and affected by our pain as well as by our joy. The process theologians will clearly answer my question, 'Can God suffer?' with a resounding 'yes'. Pittenger points out that this

> approach to God as panentheistic is closer to the facts both of scriptural teaching and of man's experience than any conception which would so exalt God metaphysically that he becomes meaningless to the life of man . . . God is closer to us than breathing, nearer than hands or feet.[3]

The process theologians and the biblical writers base their theology on the understanding of God as Love. Norman Pittenger puts it in the title of a book, *Love is the Clue.* Christians have always followed John the Evangelist in identifying God with love (agape): 'Whoever does not love does not know God, for God is love . . . No one has ever seen God, but if we love one another, God lives in union with us, and his love is made perfect in us' (1 John 4:8,12). If love is his meaning (a beautiful phrase of Julian of Norwich) then all the attributes of God are bathed in its light. God's love is all powerful, it is immovable like the rock, it is eternal.

My tenth friend gave his affirmative answer to my question after studying process theology. My own affirmative answer, 'Yes, of course God suffers' came after listening to the liberation theologians of the Third World. As my writing draws to a close I re-affirm my hope for the future of the Church, and indeed for the development of my own faith, in a God of love who doesn't abandon us, but is closer than the air we breathe. Writing this book has helped me sort out my ideas and convinced me, beyond any doubt, that my conviction lies with the liberation theologians, with the base communities and their vision of the

Church from below, a Church that truly belongs to the people. That is where I know of the presence of God, and of an authority I cannot fail to respect. I repeat here, therefore, the contrast between the two different theologies. For my weary pilgrimage has taken me from one theology to the other, with the sweat and tears that every pilgrim knows.

The two-world outlook is the traditional one. There are two worlds, one of God up there, and the other of mankind down here. God is the transcendent father who created our world, and who in his omnipotence can alter its rules if he so wills. Mankind has glimpses of God, especially in the person of Jesus, because he was sent by God down to us. Jesus is divine because he is God's own Son. Everything on earth is temporary, in fact this world is a distraction. People should live their lives with one eye always on heaven (where the Trinity dwells) for that is their true home. True riches are in heaven, and the poor and the suffering can only be comforted by being assured that they will be rewarded when they die – if they lead good lives. The reward will be eternal happiness where there is no more suffering.

The one-world view approaches God from the opposite end. All that can be known of God is known through human experience. God, the reality behind all creation, is best understood in terms of love. God is most clearly seen in the life of the human Jesus. The love and compassion he showed was unique, and leads us to call him God's own Son. God, the creator, who made people in 'his own image', is limited by his creation. People have the freedom to use their gifts for good or evil, and God cannot intervene by altering his laws. There is only one world. People are called to make it grow towards its perfection; poverty, injustice, and greed distort God's plan and prevent people from seeing God in his world.

These two theologies are literally worlds apart. The God of two-world theology cannot suffer, a view arrived at by abstract reasoning. The God of one-world theology suffers in every human suffering, a view arrived at by the experience of theologians who live alongside the poor.

If I take it from John of Damascus that none of us really

know what we are talking about, I can feel quite free to choose whichever theology speaks to my own experience. I can't prove that God suffers with us but my faith tells me that he does. It makes sense to me when I read of the heroic lives of Christians who take a preferential option for the poor in the shanty towns of Rio, or on the war-torn hillsides of El Salvador and Nicaragua, because they feel the presence of God there more powerfully than in a philosophical discussion or a theological argument. I identify with the Jesuit priest, who on taking the place of one of the murdered Jesuit priests of San Salvador, said, 'It is clear to me that God loves the little people. He is there in their poverty. He is there in their suffering.' In the sacrament of the sick we are asked to celebrate God's presence in the sick and the vulnerable, in the little people.

Resolutions for the class-room

First idea

Although I speak a great deal with my students about suffering, I am often ill at ease. I feel guilty that what I say may be just words. Many of the young people in front of me will have suffered far more than I ever have. I remember in my early days of teaching making the stupid remark, 'You are still very young so you probably won't know what it is to suffer very deeply yet.' One of the students burst into tears and fled the room. I discovered later that she had been valiantly trying to hide from everyone her situation at home. Her mother was crippled with MS and had become so difficult to live with that her father had left home. Sandra, who was preparing for her O-level exams, was rushing home to cook the meal, sometimes shop, clean the house, put on the washing, attend to her mother's needs and supervise her three younger brothers' homework. Then sit down to do hers. In the mornings she was up at 6 o'clock to do the ironing, prepare breakfast and packed lunches, and get the boys to school.

I want to avoid my early mistake at all costs. So I attempt to approach this area of teaching in more practical ways. I am wonderfully helped by the caring staff amongst whom I teach. When one girl was in hospital last term I noticed that her form-teacher arranged for two visitors to be at her bedside every single dinner hour. When a sixth-former was hospitalized, following a car crash forty miles away, the school chaplain drove frequently to see her, taking her friends with him. The same priest regularly took a group of pupils to the local hospice to visit a dying Carmelite nun. She loved their visits and the warm thoughtfulness that only the young can bring. Who else would have thought of giving her a soft, silly rabbit, which she loved to have on her bedside. 'I'd always wanted a soft toy like this as a child,' she said.

I will develop this theme of 'visiting' the sick by studying with my classes the Matthew 25 text: 'When I was sick you visited me.' One striking introduction would be to read this script from a radio talk:

> They were all sitting half dead in their wheel chairs, mostly paralysed and just existing. They didn't live. They watched some television, but if you had asked them what they had watched they probably would not have been able to tell you. We brought in a young woman who was a dancer and we told her to play beautiful old-fashioned music. She brought in Tchaikovsky records and so on, and started to dance among these old people, all in their wheel chairs which had been set in a circle. In no time the old people started to move. One old man stared at his hand and said, 'Oh, my God, I haven't moved this hand in ten years.' And the 104-year-old, in a thick German accent, said, 'That reminds me of when I danced for the Tsar of Russia.'[4]

Second idea

Last year when several of my pupils became interested in the plight of a suffering world, they opted to enter a national RE competition to express their concern for others. (They actually won the national award and went up to the House of Commons last September to receive it from the Minister of Education.) One entry by Alex highlighted the suffering of the entire Indian people of Latin America, during and since the Columbus 'invasion'. She produced a striking collage, inspired by the hunger-cloths produced by CAFOD.

I want to develop this teaching form, using the artistic skills of the children and their natural compassion for those who suffer. I won't have to look far for material for the children to use. Every day in the post the school receives requests for help from national, international and local organizations. What grief the world is carrying! One plan I have is to create an enormous cross on one school wall; it will be made into a collage of all the names and illustrations from that daily incoming literature. Classes can refer to our cross when they choose which charity their class will help.

Third idea

> I was hungry and you fed me,
> thirsty and you gave me a drink;
> I was a stranger and you received me in your homes,
> naked and you clothed me;
> I was sick and you took care of me,
> in prison and you visited me.
> The righteous will then answer him,
> 'When Lord, did we ever see you hungry and feed you?'
>
> (Matthew 25:35ff., GNB)

The Matthew text is central in our teaching; it always has been. Sometimes it becomes obvious that our Catholic children never go near church because their parents don't, and they can be a little embarrassed by RE teachers, wondering if they will tell them off. I don't see that it is my business to lay down the rules, but I do have a teacher's responsibility to explain what lies behind Catholic practice. I take the Matthew text as central to our teaching and I'm deeply aware that, when all is said and done, the Gospel doesn't mention Mass on Sundays, but it does indicate that Jesus' last word on the subject of law was his insistence that we should be concerned for those in distress.

I have several resolutions about this. Firstly, I will arrange with the art department that some pupils will produce a large, permanent mural depicting Matthew 25:35–40. When it is finished we will have it blessed during a school Mass, where my non-church-going pupils will have the opportunity to experience the strength of a community united in compassion for those in need.

Secondly, I will arrange one of our sixth-form Reflection Days around the theme of our text. I will invite a doctor or nurse, a prison chaplain or visitor, a worker from the local night-shelter, or a parishioner from the local church whose role is to welcome strangers and newcomers. During the workshop session each group will prepare a contribution to a final half-hour liturgy. With these older students I want to look more deeply into our attitudes to the underprivileged, using the following quote:

> In the first century of Christianity the hungry were fed at personal cost, the naked were clothed at personal cost, the homeless were sheltered at personal cost.
>
> And because the poor were fed, clothed and sheltered at personal cost, the pagans used to say about the Christians: 'See how they love each other.'
>
> In our own day the poor are no longer fed, clothed or sheltered at personal cost, but at the expense of the taxpayers. And because the poor are no longer fed, clothed and sheltered, the pagans say about the Christians: 'See how they pass the buck.'[5]

POSTSCRIPT: THE PILGRIM'S WAY

He who would valiant be
'gainst all disaster,
Let him in constancy
follow the master.
there's no discouragement
shall make him once relent
his first avowed intent
to be a pilgrim.

Since, Lord, thou dost defend
us with thy Spirit,
we know we at the end
shall life inherit.
Then fancies flee away!
I'll fear not what men say
I'll labour night and day
to be a pilgrim.[1]

This week my priest-cousin, Bill, arrived in Norwich with seventy other pilgrims. They had walked for two weeks from the Arundel and Brighton Diocese to the shrine of Mother Julian. We were delighted to welcome them to put down their sleeping bags on our sixth-form common-room floor. They were a merry crowd who, in true Christian style, backed up their prayer with cheerful story-telling and song in the pubs along the way.

Pilgrimage has always been an important aspect of Christian life. It is a lived-out, symbolic experience of the meaning of our lives. For life is a journey towards God, and Christ is our signpost on this journey.

I met the walking pilgrims a week ago, nearly half way into their pilgrimage and already sun-tanned but foot-sore. My brother and sister and I arrived at the country pub for lunch to surprise Bill. It was a good reunion, especially as the four of us had not been together as a foursome for years. As we sat in the garden with our ploughman's, chatting over the past, talking with young and older pilgrims and listening to Bill's enthusiastic reminiscences of earlier walking groups, I had the distinct feeling that there on that Hertfordshire lawn the conclusion to my book was being written. Bill gives his pilgrims three thoughts as they set out on their journey, and they are a perfect summary of my reflections in this book:

- Life itself is a journey.
- Rediscover what lies at the heart of things.
- God is found *in carne*, in a human community.

Life itself is a journey

I took this as the actual theme of my book: the weary teacher/pilgrim moving on, often painfully, from landmark to landmark. I looked at baptism in chapter 1, the start of the journey that involves a lifelong process of growing, developing and eventually maturing, which I analysed in chapter 4 on confirmation. Anyone who has been on a touring holiday which means no more than two nights in any one spot will appreciate the frustrations of living out of a suitcase. Our pilgrims roll up their bedding each day, pack their rucksack and move on to the next place. Life, we say as Christians, should be like that. It will be full of insecurity; we will often want to stop still and put down roots. But if we stay too long in one place we will never reach the goal.

I reflected in chapters 1 and 4 on a Church that seems to have put down such firm roots that it has become unfaithful to its pilgrim character. I expressed my great distress at the divided Christendom where denominations have become so immovable in their own traditions that the possibility of unity seems only a wild dream. However, in this final reflection I must record that there are times when I am filled with optimism and hope. Were this not so I would have given up long ago. I noted with pleasure that Bill's pilgrims were a great mixture of Catholics and non-Catholics, and were quite naturally sharing the richness of their faith with each other.

I have also learnt while writing this book (recording things does seem to sharpen the impact of events), that circumstances can change very quickly. I wrote in chapter 1, six months ago, that my father and I could hardly communicate over my mother's death. That has changed: time has healed him. I wrote that my nephew was denied a place in the Catholic school. That has changed too, by the intervention, I suspect, of a more sympathetic priest.

Journeys are unpredictable; around the next corner of the road there can be a monstrous hold-up. On the other hand, there may be a most glorious view of the distant goal. Teaching is like that too. Alongside my agonies, struggles and obstacles as an RE teacher, I've pointed out the unexpected bonuses and joys – the sheer pleasure of sharing at depth with young, eager minds. The aim of course, of every teacher is to see the pupils walk on ahead. And they do.

Every pilgrimage journey needs enormous preparation and leadership. Bill shared with us his years of experience and the conclusion he has reached. I could link everything he said to chapter 5 on 'Who's in charge?' There I expressed my concern and dissatisfaction with the style of church leadership. Trained and commissioned under a hierarchical regime, it is hardly surprising that my cousin began his pilgrimage work as the organizer, leader, do-it-all man. Over the years, by growing to experience the fact that the community is the Church, Bill has stepped back, and given over the pilgrimage to the people. We sat and had our lunch with him while others organized the next phase of the journey. Bill listened to and joined in, setting off on the afternoon walk somewhere towards the back. I set my eyes for home warmed by the vision of a pilgrim Church, young and old, Christian rather than Catholic, cheerfully stepping out, led by the laity but strengthened and enabled by a leader who listened and laughed a lot.

Rediscover what lies at the heart of things

Materialistic values mean rather little on a pilgrim journey. Pilgrims can discover a new joy in living, for a time, with a minimum of comforts, in the support of a sharing community. It is good to shed from time to time some of the trappings with which we have surrounded ourselves. We go on and on collecting unnecessary things, which in the end obscure the heart of the matter. I personally am very bad at not letting go of things. I had to spend the whole day in school recently just to clear one small cupboard where I had accumulated so much 'might be useful' objects that I had totally hidden some very helpful teaching aids that I could have used last term.

I touched on this matter when I discussed the Eucharist in chapter 2. There I analysed the problem of religious language which all too often obscures the heart of the matter. Over centuries of theological bickering, the Church has often shrouded gospel truths with language so obscure that we are in danger of missing the real Christ. If he is my signpost to God I need to know him in the Eucharist and in his body, the community. I want to see and know him clearly, uncluttered by the baggage of centuries.

When people live the poverty of a pilgrim they are thrown closer together. They need each other to survive. I noticed that several people on that pub lawn were helping one another to soothe their blistered feet. I was told that the accompanying van was picking up one girl who had twisted her ankle. She would be carried to the next stopping-place to give her foot time to heal. I discussed healing in chapter 3 where I looked at the extent to which healing lies within the scope of the whole community. For Bill's pilgrims, the presence of that van to carry all the heavier burdens and go on ahead to welcome the walkers to their resting places, must be a great comfort. The Church is a community in which help and comfort is always at hand. That also is part of the heart of the matter.

God is found in carne, *in a human community*

This, above all, summarizes what I have tried to say in this book. I am so convinced of the real humanity of Christ, my signpost to God, that (to repeat it for the last time) I make this the basis of all my teaching. I tell my pupils over and over again that we can find God in the ordinariness of a human life like that of Jesus. When ordinary human love, forgiveness and compassion are shown, God is present. We look at the human Jesus, and know God.

So in chapter 6 I wanted to demolish the terrible blasphemy which holds that marriage is only a second-best option for Christians. There are no special, chosen people who are given greater intimacy with God than others. We are all invited to come into the presence of God as we hold the hands of his Son, Jesus, and do not refuse to continue holding it when it leads to the cross.

Suffering is therefore part of this incarnational package. The sacrament of the sick is a special gift of the Church, for it offers the hope and consolation of the healing Christ who accompanies us on the pilgrimage. But as I emphasized in chapter 7, it is we who are the hands and heart of Christ. We must heal one another.

Readers will know by now that my vision for the Church of the future lies in the renewed life of Christians who experience God by taking the 'option for the poor'. It is they who have taught me most clearly to turn from a two-world theology to a one-world expression of the mystery that we call God. What I have come to experience of my Christian faith as a wife, mother and teacher is best expressed for me in the language of liberation theology. Whatever frightening obstacle may be round the next corner of the road I tread, I am able to keep going because I know that the community of fellow pilgrims gives me the strength to keep following Jesus. I may have criticized my weary Roman Catholic Church in these pages, but I do not love her any the less. I may sigh some very heavy sighs when I look at the Vatican, but I take heart from my knowledge that the Vatican is a very minor part of the Church. The Church of the poor clears my vision, and as I stand alongside these fellow pilgrims in Rome, I join my voice to the Nicaraguan bishop who wrote these lines:

> I, sinner and bishop, confess to arriving in Rome
> with my rural crook,
> taking the colonnades by surprise
> and practising my panpipes to drown out the sound of the organ;
> to having arrived in Assisi, circled about by poppies.
> I, sinner and bishop, confess to dreaming of a Church
> clothed only in the Gospel and sandals;
> to believing in the Church,
> sometimes even in spite of the Church,
> to believing in the Kingdom,
> in any case, walking in the Church.
> I, sinner and bishop, confess to having seen Jesus of Nazareth
> announcing the Good News to the poor of Latin America;
> to saying to Mary 'Hail, mother and friend of all!'
> to celebrating the blood of those who have been faithful;
> to being a pilgrim.
> I, sinner and bishop, confess to loving Nicaragua, a child of the times.
> I, sinner and bishop, confess to opening the window of time every morning;
> to speaking to others like brother to brother
> to never losing my dream, my song, my laugh;
> to cultivating the flower of hope amidst the wounds of the Risen One.[2]

❧

NOTES

1: Making a New Start

1. The headings for the chapters are taken from H. J. Richards, *The Sacraments for Children* (McCrimmons 1988).
2. 'Laudato Sii, O mi Signore', *Hymns Old and New* No. 294, Damian Lundy (Kevin Mayhew 1989).
3. 'Do not be Afraid', *Songs of the Spirit*, No. 38, Gerard Markland (Kevin Mayhew 1978).
4. P. Tillich, *The Shaking of the Foundations* (London 1949).

2: Feed the World

1. *Catechism of Christian Doctrine* (Catholic Truth Society, 1958), p. 47.
2. *Hymns Old and New,* No. 72 (Kevin Mayhew 1989), my italics.
3. D. Hilton, *Liturgy of Life*, No. 157 (National Christian Education Council 1991). The poem is described as 'anonymous' but was in fact written by Frances Croake Frank.
4. J. D. Rayner, *Passover Haggadah* (Union of Liberal and Progressive Synagogues 1981).
5. P. Wilkinson, *Focus on the Sacraments* (Kevin Mayhew 1987).
6. H. Lavery, *Sacraments* (Darton, Longman and Todd 1982), p. 44.
7. *Liturgy of Life*, op cit., No. 171.

3: Trespassers Will Be Forgiven

1. *Catechism of Christian Doctrine* (Catholic Truth Society 1958), p. 21.
2. N. Farber, *Christian Century,* 1 July 1970.
3. P. Wilkinson, *Focus on the Sacraments* (Kevin Mayhew 1987), p. 41.
4. D. Chorley, Letter to *Catholic Herald*, 3 April 1987.
5. *Repent and Believe* (Catholic Truth Society 1984), p. 5.
6. P. Wilkinson, *Focus on the Sacraments* (Kevin Mayhew 1987), p. 49.

4: Growing Up

1. 'Viewpoint', *The Tablet*, 10 February 1990.
2. CAFOD literature for schools.
3. Kairos Statement, *Road to Damascus* (CIIR 1989).
4. *Documents of Vatican II: Church in the Modern World* (Geoffrey Chapman 1966).
5. J. Cortina SJ, *The Faith of Archbishop Romero* (CIIR 1986).
6. J. Fuchs, *Moral Theology Renewed* (Furrow/Gill 1965).
7. F. Turner, *How Can We Create a Just Society?* (Darton, Longman and Todd 1992).
8. P. De Rosa, *A Bible Prayer Book for Today* (Fontana/Collins 1976), p. 81.

5: By Whose Authority?

1. P. Wilkinson, *Focus on the Sacraments* (Kevin Mayhew 1987), p. 76.
2. P. Purnell SJ, *Our Faith Story* (Collins 1985), p. 29.
3. D. Soelle, *Celebrating Resistance* (Mowbray 1993).

6: God is Love

1. D. Soelle, *Celebrating Resistance* (Mowbray 1993).
2. P. Purnell SJ, *Our Faith Story* (Collins 1985), p. 111.

7: You Did It Unto Me

1. P. Wilkinson, *Focus on the Sacraments* (Kevin Mayhew 1987), p. 53.
2. S. Cassidy, *Good Friday People* (Darton, Longman and Todd 1991), p. 116.
3. N. Pittenger, *God in Process* (SCM 1967), p. 17.
4. *The Listener* (taken from D. Hilton, *Liturgy of Life*, No. 167).
5. Peter Maurin in *Easy Essays* (available from Catholic Worker Farm, Route 1, Box 308, West Hamlin, W. Virginia, VA 25571, USA – Copyright free).

Postcript: The Pilgrim's Way

1. Percy Dearmer (1867–1936), 'Pilgrim's Hymn', after John Bunyan (1628–88).
2. Dom Pedro Casaldaliga, *Continent of Hope* (CAFOD 1993), p. 27.